INCREASING
STUDENT
MOTIVATION

INCREASING
STUDENT
MOTIVATION

Strategies for
Middle
and
High School
Teachers

Margaret A. Theobald

CORWIN PRESS
A SAGE Publications Company
Thousand Oaks, California

For information:

Corwin Press
A Sage Publications Company
2455 Teller Road
Thousand Oaks, California 91320
www.corwinpress.com

Sage Publications Ltd.
1 Oliver's Yard
55 City Road
London EC1Y 1SP
United Kingdom

Sage Publications India Pvt. Ltd.
B-42, Panchsheel Enclave
Post Box 4109
New Delhi 110 017 India

Printed in the United States of America.

Library of Congress Cataloging-in-Publication Data

Theobald, Margaret A.
Increasing student motivation: Strategies for middle and high school teachers / Margaret A. Theobald.
     p. cm.
Includes bibliographical references and index.
ISBN 1-4129-0622-9 (cloth)—ISBN 1-4129-0623-7 (pbk.)
   1. Motivation in education. 2. Middle school teaching. 3. High school teaching. I. Title.
LB1065.T46 2006
370.154—dc22   2005009585

This book is printed on acid-free paper.

05 06 07 08 09 10 9 8 7 6 5 4 3 2 1

Acquisitions Editor:	Elizabeth Brenkus
Editorial Assistants:	Candice L. Ling and Jingle Vea
Production Editor:	Laureen Shea
Copy Editor:	Rachel Hile Bassett
Typesetter:	C&M Digitals (P) Ltd.
Proofreader:	Penelope Sippel
Indexer:	Nara Wood
Cover Designer:	Rose Storey
Illustrator:	Christina L. Theobald

Contents

Foreword

The concerned teacher said, "I have tried everything and I just cannot seem to find a way to engage John in American history! What can I do?" The principal's reply involved a series of "did you try this?" and "did you try that?" questions. The brief conversation ended with little assistance for the excellent teacher, who was seeking to find a way to *motivate* her student(s) to be successful. As a busy middle school principal, I can attest to the reality of this hypothetical conversation with a number of excellent teachers and the inadequacy of time to address each concern.

In this book, *Increasing Student Motivation: Strategies for Middle and High School Teachers*, Dr. Margaret (Margie) Theobald succinctly identifies various motivational techniques which provide teachers with alternatives to implement as an answer to the hypothetical question above. Dr. Theobald identifies specific strategies which are centered around the creation of a positive, personal environment for learning for the "action-oriented" students of the 21st century. For example, she encourages teachers to provide action alternatives including "designing a floor plan for a house" or "creating a new lab experiment for a science class." As I read the book, her choice of action words for the teacher's role in utilizing the suggested alternatives is indicative of the role of the teacher. Amongst these the teacher should "provide," "allow," "ask," "involve," "help," "expect," "assign," "encourage," "give," "offer," and "teach"—referring both to teaching how to meet expectations as well as teaching content.

This book provides a wonderful resource for busy teachers, harried principals, and school improvement teams searching for methods designed to enhance the achievement of all students by providing them with tools for lifelong learning. Her approach to teaching is student focused and involves the engagement of students in the learning process.

Margie's academic background, which includes graduate degrees in her teaching area, secondary administration, and curriculum and instruction, combined with her experience as a middle school teacher and college professor, have given her a personal, firsthand opportunity to develop and implement multiple motivational strategies for her students. In addition, other professional experiences involving publication of educational literature including books, numerous articles, textbook reviews, as well as multiple presentations and workshops have exposed Dr. Theobald to the very best in current philosophy and implementation of the teaching act. She espouses the concept of student empowerment and responsibility. She believes that students must be involved in all aspects of their education. I have personally attended several of Margie's presentations over the years at both state and national conferences and have read many of the articles that she has written, and I recall her focus on student motivation.

I believe that this book fills an important niche in educational literature and will prove to be an invaluable resource for teachers, principals, and other educational personnel who work with students and are concerned about how to help students maximize their potential. With this book as a resource, the principal mentioned at the beginning of this foreword will have a resource to utilize in providing alternatives when caring teachers come with questions and concerns. In this day of increased accountability, maximizing student performance is a significant goal. This book helps to address significant issues related to student achievement.

—John A. Pohl, EdD

Retired Principal, Pattonville School District
St. Louis County, Missouri

Former President of the Missouri Middle School Association

National Middle School Association Principal of the Year, 1990

Colleague and friend of the author
through the Missouri Middle School Association

Acknowledgments

Sincere and grateful thanks are not nearly enough in expressing what I feel about the support and guidance provided by my dear friend and professional colleague, Dr. Sheila R. Caskey. This book might never have been completed without her inspiration and the belief and support she continually provided me during the writing of this manuscript. Sheila's constant source of energy and her limitless patience, not to mention the donation of her keyboarding skills, were motivating factors in my ability to complete this book ahead of schedule. My thanks to her are limitless.

I extend my appreciation and admiration to my two younger nieces. To Melissa A. Theobald, for assisting me in creating a video on student motivation during the earlier stages of research for this book, I thank her so much for her time and patience, and for putting herself on camera for all the teachers through the years with whom I shared this video. To Christina L. Theobald, for sharing her prodigious artistic talents in creating the thematic character "Mo" (for motivation) who appears in each of her 10 illustrations in this book, a heartfelt thank-you. It was fun working with her on this project. Her enthusiasm helped keep me motivated to complete the manuscript.

My appreciation extends to my friend and professional colleague, Dr. John A. Pohl for taking time out of his busy retirement schedule to read an early draft of the manuscript and write the foreword. John spent his professional working years making education a motivating experience for young adolescents. He has my respect and admiration for being an effective educator and a really nice human being.

Thank you to three professional colleagues who were willing to take the time to read the manuscript and submit their reviews directly to the publisher. To Mr. Art Dickinson (teacher, Perryville High School, Perryville, Missouri), Dr. David Waters (principal, Farmington High School, Farmington, Missouri), and Dr. Ada Cruce (counselor-educator, Southeast Missouri State University), thank you for the time spent in this venture.

To my former and present teacher education students as well as all my teacher friends, thank you for your continued belief in and use of motivating practices with the adolescents in our schools and for sharing some of those practices with me through the years. May you continue to create the environments in your schools that will help motivate students to succeed.

I am grateful to the editors at Corwin Press, whose constant availability and support helped lead this project to publication; to Robb Clouse, for his support in moving the initial proposal to a contract; to Elizabeth Brenkus, for being available to answer my naive questions and address my concerns along the way and for all her time in editing the manuscript; and to Candice Ling, for picking up the pieces and fragments necessary in the publication business. I thank all of you.

And, to Ms. Diana Heck, friend and professional colleague, who told me over 30 years ago that someday I would be a "doctor" and write a book . . . well, with that motivating challenge, Diana, here's the book!

Corwin Press gratefully acknowledges the contributions of the following individuals:

Lauren Baah, Teacher
Irving High School
Irving, TX

Carrie Carpenter, Teacher
Hugh Hartman Middle School
Redmond, OR

Ada L. Cruce, Professor Emeritus
Southeast Missouri State
    University
Cape Girardeau, MO

Art Dickinson, High School
    Physical Education Teacher
Perry County School District #32
Perryville, MO

Daniel Elliott, Author,
    Associate Professor
School of Education and
    Behavioral Studies
Azusa Pacific University
Azusa, CA

Kathleen Falcetta, National Board
    Certified Teacher
Granville Elementary School
Granville, NY

Ruth Ann Gharst, Teacher
Cedar Creek Elementary School
Olathe, KS

Barbara Hayhurst, Teacher
Central Canyon
    Elementary School
Nampa, ID

Janet Hurt, Associate
    Superintendent for
    Curriculum & Instruction
Logan County Board
    of Education
Russellville, KY

Mark Merrell, Principal
James Madison High School
Vienna, VA

Robert W. Pickett, Teacher
Marion Elementary School
Sheridan, IN

Deborah L. Smith, Teacher
Glencliff Elementary School
Nashville, TN

Judith Smock, Teacher
Clark Elementary School
Erie, PA

David L. Waters, Principal
Farmington Senior High School
Farmington, MO

Cathie West, Principal
Mountain Way Elementary School
Granite Falls, WA

About the Author

 **Margaret A. Theobald, EdD,** has been at Southeast Missouri State University for the past 24 years and is a Professor in the Department of Middle and Secondary Education. She was a teacher at the middle and high school levels for more than 15 years in both public and parochial schools in Illinois and Missouri. She earned her doctorate in Curriculum and Instruction at Illinois State University with an emphasis on education at the middle school level. She has served in several positions with the Missouri Middle School Association and its executive board, including the offices of secretary and president. Her research includes a statewide survey of middle-level practices and trends. The Missouri Middle School Association published the results of this survey in its 1994 *Missouri Middle Level Practices and Trends: A Resource Directory.* She was also coauthor for the 1995 publication *The Middle School Principal* (Corwin Press). She has made numerous presentations at both the state and national levels and has published several articles. Her most recent research has been in the area of teaching strategies and student motivation. This book is the result of a two-decade-long interest in these topics and represents the culmination of her career as a teacher educator.

This book is dedicated to my mom, Mary Ann "Marion" Theobald, who, during the first 13 years of my life, provided the motivating environment that allowed me to learn by doing, trying new things, and making mistakes in the process; and who, when I did err, demonstrated the unconditional love that motivated me to keep trying. It is her spirit that inspired me through my challenging teen years, sustained me through my career as a teacher, and to this day continues to provide me with the intrinsic motivation to be true to myself.

Introduction

If America's only educational duty were to educate everyone who is anxious and willing to learn, we could close down half our schools.

—William F. Buckley, Jr. (as cited in Shanley, 1990)

Herein lies the challenge for teachers: to help students become motivated enough to learn and eager enough to continue to learn and succeed beyond the formal years of schooling. Motivation is internal; it comes from within oneself. A student who is not motivated and does not want to learn cannot be made to learn. One of the greatest challenges for teachers in the 21st century is to provide an environment and atmosphere that can stimulate a student's desire to learn. This task is especially complex because of the numerous variables that affect a student's motivation and because of the differences that students bring to the school environment.

Some of these differences include cognitive abilities, home environment, personal physical challenges, and especially differences that directly relate to the student's culture. Wlodkowski (1999) said that "individual motivation is inseparable from culture" (p. 8). Therefore, effective teachers must continually seek ways to manipulate the learning environment in order to maximize the motivational levels of individual students to learn as well as address the social ramifications and instructional needs resulting from differences in culture. The ultimate goal is to help all students succeed during their years of schooling so that they will also succeed throughout their adult years.

In theory, there are two general types of motivation, extrinsic and intrinsic. *Extrinsic motivation* refers to the external influences of praise and rewards. For some students, extrinsic tools are necessary for motivation. This might eventually lead to a level of motivation that is intrinsic. *Intrinsic motivation* refers to the internal drive within oneself to do well because of a desire to be challenged, for the sheer joy of participating or learning, or because of a personal desire to succeed. Certainly, the development and nurturing of intrinsic motivation is the ultimate goal of educators for their students. Wlodkowski (1982) said that intrinsic motivation occurs when there is value in the process of doing something. Helping students find value in learning through the implementation of various instructional strategies and multiple alternative and authentic forms of assessments, while maintaining high standards of student performance in an environment which encourages students to do their best work by effective, nurturing teachers, will help increase the motivational levels of all students.

In an effort to provide practical suggestions teachers might use to help create an environment for students to maintain or increase internal motivation to learn, this book offers many suggestions. The professional literature abounds with theories of learning that affect a student's level of motivation. This book offers a snapshot of those relevant theories that provide some foundation for students' motivation. While the book contains references to enduring motivational theories such as those of Maslow (1954, 1968), Gagné (1965, 1974), and Bandura (1977), the root of the strategies and suggestions lies in the experiences of the author and the hundreds of teachers who have worked with her preservice students over the past decade.

This book is not intended to provide all the answers to issues of student apathy, disinterest, and lack of motivation to learn, but rather, the strategies and suggestions in this book are offered as a springboard for teachers in developing and implementing ideas that might be useful for them and their students. Because students are individuals and motivation is an internal, personal attribute, some strategies and suggestions that work for some students will not work for others. Not everything will work for every person.

The strategies in this book were written primarily for middle and high school teachers for use with adolescents. However, this is not to say that elementary school teachers and even college professors would not benefit by adapting some of these ideas for students at these respective academic levels.

Each chapter has strategies and suggestions that relate to a theme that is suggested by a letter in the word motivation. Chapter 1 explores strategies related to one's "mindset." Adolescents come into their classes with an already established mindset as to whether or not they can succeed. Chapter 2 offers suggestions for establishing a motivating environment centered on the theme of "observation." Adolescents are influenced by what they see and observe in others, especially their teachers. Chapter 3 suggests that students may be affected by "timing." Maslow's (1954) theory of motivation provides the foundation for the strategies in this chapter.

Students' needs and readiness influence their levels of motivation. In Chapter 4, the theme of "independence" is offered. Teaching students to write goals for themselves, make their own decisions, and recognize consequences for those decisions provides the focus for strategies in this chapter. The fact that students are motivated by their own successes provides the theme of "victory" for Chapter 5. Some students have never experienced success. The strategies in this chapter are for them. Students, especially adolescents, need to be active learners, and Chapter 6 contains suggestions centered on "action" strategies. One of the goals for student learning is that students be able to "transfer" information when needed. Chapter 7 provides numerous suggestions related to this process of transference. Chapter 8 contains strategies related to "individuality." Each student is unique and is affected by the environment differently than anyone else. In Chapter 9, taking responsibility for one's own actions provides the theme for "ownership" strategies. The essence of motivation is actually an internal need reflected in ownership and responsibility. Chapter 10 provides strategies that revolve around the theme that motivation is "natural." All persons have an innate drive that motivates their actions.

For new teachers as well as those with some experience in the realm of educating students, this book offers strategies and suggestions that you might find directly adoptable for you and your students. Or, you might modify a suggestion or develop your own slant on an idea from this book. In any case, I sincerely hope that in reading these ideas, you find some benefit from my sharing them.

1 Motivation Is a Mindset

The mind is master of the man, and so, "They can who think they can!"

—Nexon Waterman (as cited in Shanley, 1990)

By the time students reach their middle school years, they already have a mindset about who they are and what they can or cannot accomplish. Edwards (1954) and Atkinson (1964) developed theories of motivation related to a person's expectations of the value of success based on that person's perceived probability of succeeding and the incentive value of that success. In an article in the August 15, 1993, issue of *Parade*, Jimmy Johnson, who was then coach of the Dallas Cowboys, was asked how he turned a team with a losing record into Super Bowl champions. He simply said, "Treat them as winners . . . and they will win." In the school environment, if students believe they can be successful, they usually are. If students believe they cannot succeed, then students probably will not and will have little to no motivation to do otherwise. Glasser (1990) said that motivation comes from within ourselves.

Teachers can affect in several ways the mindset that individual students bring with them into the school setting. First, teachers need to recognize that each student can learn. I have heard skeptics scoff at this notion, but each student enrolled in a school can learn. It is just the capacity of learning that varies among students.

Second, teachers are responsible for providing an environment where students can feel free to make mistakes and learn from those mistakes. Sometimes the most significant learning takes place when students have the opportunity to correct their errors.

Third, everyone needs positive feedback once in a while. Students need to know that teachers appreciate them for who they are and what they can do. Teachers can comment on qualities, strengths, and positive characteristics of their students.

Fourth, in addition to the preceding suggestions, teachers can provide opportunities for students to increase self-esteem and enhance a positive self-concept. This, in turn, will help students develop the confidence needed to be successful.

EACH STUDENT LEARNS

Each student can learn. The challenge for teachers is to figure out what kinds of teaching strategies work for the students in any given class. Getting to know students as individuals is critical to recognizing how each student can best learn. Several practical suggestions for accomplishing this follow.

Tie in relevant, current issues directly to your students.

Connect issues of the times to the social lives of your students. Students need to recognize and find relevance to their own lives in what you are teaching. If students can make a connection to what they already know about in their lives and experiences, it is more likely they will be interested in what you have to say. For instance, any issue related to economics is important to adolescents when you make a connection to the cost of purchasing and maintaining a car. Income tax and social security become realities when students work and their take-home pay is not what they expected. The hidden challenge here is that as an educator, you need to know about adolescents in the 2000s and what the foci of their lives are.

Allow independent work on self-chosen topics when related to general goals.

When students are allowed to have choices, they will pick topics that are of interest to them. If certain topics interest students, they will find more meaning and application and will ultimately retain concepts for transfer and generalizability later. Consider the basic example of the student who does not like to read anything except books about airplanes. If reading is the goal, continued encouragement to read books on airplanes can lead to reading more about aerodynamics, geometry, physics, and other related academic areas.

Recognize students individually.

This does not have to take much time. Just find a moment when you can look a student in the eye and recognize that the student exists. Sometimes just a comment about how tired the student may look that day can lead to more insight on your part about that student. Just recently (as a matter of fact, it was the first day of class) one of my college students looked as though he was ready to fall asleep in class. He could not keep his eyes open, and he was sitting in front of the class right before me. When I said something to him about how tired he looked, he apologized and explained he had not gotten much sleep. It turns out the student was a Community Adviser in one of the college residence halls and had spent most of the night dealing with "Freshmanitis" and its resultant chaotic activities. Just let students know you recognize them as individuals.

Provide equal opportunities for each student. Generate the feeling that everyone is on the same page.

Point out to students that they are each about the same age, same level of life experience, same "grade" level. Sometimes adolescents, particularly the "younger" ones, are so preoccupied with life and the challenges it presents that they fail to see that they are not alone. Other students are experiencing similar feelings and situations. Once in a while I used to ask my students how many of them had felt or experienced whatever topic was at hand. When a student sees the upraised hands of other students who are in the same situation, it makes the student feel better to realize that he or she is not alone.

Ignore student names on tests or quizzes and other similar tasks.

Have students put their names on the back side of their work. (Sure you can peek, but that will not help.) As teachers, we can be influenced by which student's work we are reading or evaluating. Be more objective and evaluate the student's work, rather than the individual student. You may be surprised to find that students you perceive to do well may indeed demonstrate difficulty at times, and some students whose work you perceive more negatively may fully comprehend and demonstrate abilities you did not expect.

Recognize new days, every day.

Accept that each day begins anew, and teach your students to recognize this also. This is especially important following a day of challenges, a day that seemed to be twice as long a school day as others. Teach students through your own attitude that the sun rises each day and a fresh beginning presents itself every 24 hours. Say so. Be up front about new opportunities every day. Like the old saying goes: The past is history, the future is yet to be, and all we have is the present.

Recognize that there are different degrees of motivation.

This is true, especially across content areas. For instance, a student might be more interested in math than language arts. Your job is to figure out what piques the interests of your students and what does not. You are an adult. You do not have the same degree of interest in everything in life, so why should you expect your students to like every subject they study in school? Recognize this and let your students know that you appreciate varying levels of interest on their part. Then, help students develop at least an appreciation for the importance of studying *all* subjects in school. Help them learn to enjoy their most interesting subjects and also learn more about others.

Make up your own mind about students and their abilities.

Refrain from listening to others and their opinions about students. Sometimes we can be influenced about students by what other teachers have to say. Admit it. Be independent enough to get to know your students yourself. You might find redeeming characteristics in your students and share these positive qualities with your colleagues.

Ignore stereotypes.

Let a student's performance represent what a student can do, rather than be influenced by "labels." It has almost gotten to the point in our society that a student is unique if the student fails to have a "label" (ADHD, LD, behavior disorder [BD], etc.). Let students demonstrate what they can do rather than letting a "label" tell you what to expect.

Keep personal preferences to yourself.

Teachers are in schools for all students. We meet people in life we naturally gravitate toward because of common interests, personality type, and so on. So, it is natural that teachers would "like" some students more than others. As an educator, you have to be careful that your actions and attitudes convey impartial attitudes toward all students. You are an educator for *all* students in your classes.

Consider that you have individual students with their own learning styles in your classes.

There are so many theories about learning styles that you might want to throw in the towel altogether. Hang in there. Just consider that students have different strengths and we need to capitalize on those strengths. For instance, I am a visual and kinesthetic learner. That takes my mind out of it if you were to lecture to me without adding any visual stimuli. So what do you think happens with your students? Just take the basic three styles— auditory, visual, kinesthetic, and combinations—and start from there to find ways to address the different learning styles of your various students. You might want to ask students or take inventory of how your students learn best. (See Resource A for a cross-reference of instructional strategies based on student learning styles.) In addition, there are Web sites that allow students to input their own learning preferences and the sites will automatically analyze this information for a resultant learning style. Go to www.idpride.net. You can also go to www.howtolearn.com and click on Personal Learning Styles Inventory. If you want to use the latter site with your students, you will need to obtain a site license. The Web site explains how to obtain the license.

Provide clearly stated objectives.

Students will perform closer to our expectations if we let them know exactly what those expectations are. It is sometimes clear in our heads what we want students to do and how to do it, but sometimes students are not clear about the same. Write objectives out so students can see them and hear them at the same time. Put all tasks and behaviors in clear terms. Let students know you want them to list, define, outline, analyze, critique, and so on. Tell students exactly what you want them to do.

Set guidelines and communicate those guidelines for work to students.

Students want and need to know how you expect work to be presented. If you do not tell students, maybe they will ask and maybe not. Your job is to be clear and consistent about the conditions related to an assignment or task. Tell students if you want them to use a computer, work by themselves, use the book, and how long or involved the task should be. Tell students what is acceptable. Giving students clear guidelines lets them know under what conditions you will accept their work. But this is not the same as what the qualitative or evaluative part of their work should be. Make this distinction for students: These are the conditions or guidelines that must be met *before* you will evaluate student work.

Set objectives so students can be successful.

Let students know the degree of acceptance for their work. What exactly will be evaluated? Is it more important to have a certain number of pages, or is it the qualitative and thoughtful ideas reflected in a student's work that will be "graded"? Students need to know this! Make the distinction between "conditions" of acceptability (work must be neat, typed, or students must have worked by themselves, etc.) and what is "evaluated" (the qualitative element of the work the student submits).

Try using "wacky" anticipatory sets!

Sure, it takes time and effort to come up with a good anticipatory set or introduction to a lesson, something that will catch the students' attention and get them excited about what you are about to teach. So, take the time to prepare a "wacky" one once in a while and see what happens. Dress up, or have someone from your local historical society dress up as Abraham Lincoln and see what difference it makes in student attention to the Civil War lesson. Bring a pizza to class and slice it up in front of the group. Then tell students you want to talk about fractions. You might even enlist a small group of students to come up with a good "set" for the next unit. You might be surprised with what students can create! This may get them more interested in the unit topic. Once students are interested, they will be motivated to learn more. See Robin Hunter's 2004 updated edition of *Madeline Hunter's Mastery Teaching* for more examples.

Start teaching and learning with what students already know.

Use a strategy like K-W-L—what students already Know, what they Want to find out, and what they would like to Learn (Carr & Ogle, 1987; Ogle, 1986)—to help control boredom and help you set objectives for learning. Students who already know about the topic you are teaching can be further challenged or utilized to share their knowledge with other students. Sometimes students will be more motivated to learn from one another. Using Bloom's taxonomy (Bloom, Englehart, Furst, Hill, & Krathwohl, 1956) you can then set appropriate objectives at various levels of challenge for students. (See Resource B for an outline of this taxonomy.)

Implement new and different teaching strategies.

Teachers try to find their comfort zones when it comes to how they teach and what they do. But, the teacher's comfort zone for teaching may not be the comfort zone for student learning. Because students learn in various ways, teachers should teach in various ways. The learning environment will be more exciting for everyone! Try new and different ways of teaching, and let students in on it. As a teacher, you are not in this alone. Let students know when you have never done a new strategy before; and tell students that if it works, you will do it again. If it does not work, you will fix it or scrap it altogether. Then let students help you decide whether or not you repeat this new strategy. You may find that students were more engaged during the activity than you expected because they knew they would have a say in whether you might use this strategy again. Talk to other teachers about what works for them and adapt strategies for yourself. Be open to trying different approaches. You may be surprised to find how well a new strategy works when you are willing to take a risk and try something you have never done before.

Vary your methods of assessment.

Because students learn in various ways, students ought to be allowed to demonstrate *what* they have learned in various ways. I am an organized and visually stimulated person. So, I enjoy and am motivated to accomplish tasks that allow me to demonstrate these characteristics (portfolios, scrapbooks, charts, diagrams, etc.). A friend of mine who is a physical educator wanted students to know and understand the health- and skill-related components of physical fitness. He had one student use a foam board to draw a diagram of these components and then cut the entire diagram into several pieces, creating a jigsaw puzzle that could be used by other students as reinforcement. Another one of his students wrote a poem demonstrating her understanding of health- and skill-related components of physical fitness. Both of these assessment activities were evidence for what students learned. Keep an open mind to accepting various methods of assessment.

Focus on each student's positive characteristics.

You may not know what the positive characteristics of each student might be because they are not obvious. So, ask your students. Have students write or talk about themselves and indicate what they are most proud of and what they would change about themselves if they could. This reminds me of the strategies that teachers used back in the late 1960s and early 1970s in values clarification (Simon, Howe, & Kirschenbaum, 1972). It might help to revisit these and make applications to students of the 2000s. Students' interests and ideas change over time, but basic human characteristics remain constant.

Affecting the mindset of students begins with you.

Share your own experiences with students, such as a time when you were not sure you could do something, but then you tried and found that you could be successful. Continually point out that success begins with one's mindset. If you think you cannot, you probably will not. If you think you can, you might find success. Remind students about the childhood story of *The Little Engine That Could* (Piper, 1990).

Let students help with making their own rules for grading.

Teach students about evaluative criteria, grading scales, scoring guides, and rubrics. They take much time to design. Let students help do this. They will understand to a greater degree what you are expecting of them. Besides, if students take part in some decision making, they will find ownership in it and be more interested and motivated to work.

Get to know your students' names and interests.

Nothing gets a student more interested in learning than a teacher calling that student by name, or relating something in the teaching episode to an interest of that student. But, how can you do this if you do not know your students to begin with? You can do several things at the beginning of the year. Take time to have students introduce themselves to one another and point out something relevant about themselves (what they are most proud of, what accomplishment they achieved during the summer, something new they have learned, something that they feel is "unique" to themselves). This will help review their names for you as well as give you additional information about each student. I sometimes have students write me a letter. I ask for specific information like birth order in the family, what students like to do in their free time and why, what skills they have that they feel are really good, and what skills are not very good that they feel they need to improve. Then, I can collect these letters and read them at a later time. I often refer back to these letters every so often during the year to remind myself about the lives and interests of my students.

Use interest inventories to help students learn more about themselves.

Sometimes students do not know what their strengths are, or what they are really interested in. There are several interest inventories available (look in the reference sections of your local library, search the Internet, ask your local guidance counselor) that do not take a lot of time to complete in the classroom, but would help your students in the long run to identify their strengths and interests. This alone can provide students with motivation to learn.

MISTAKES AID LEARNING

Sometimes learning takes place when we make mistakes. Consider the fact that errors frequently occur when adults attempt to assemble products before reading the directions. The resulting product often turns out much differently than anticipated. Only then are we ready to learn. The same type of learning occurs with students. However, the environment in school needs to be such that students feel free to make mistakes and then to be able to correct those mistakes. Consider the following suggestions and choose what works for you.

Let students resubmit their work.

Students need to work toward mastery and should have an opportunity to correct mistakes and learn from them. There are limits though! Consider what students do with their work after a "grade" is affixed.

Many students "file" work on their way out of the classroom. What difference would it make if you pointed out errors and allowed students to correct them before being evaluated for a grade? In life, we all learn from our mistakes. In school, it is the same for students. If they know they have a chance to "fix" their errors and resubmit their work, you might find students more motivated to try. Oh sure, I have read all the controversy about allowing students to redo their work. But, really, what is the formative stage of learning all about anyway?

Use green, purple, or turquoise colored pens.

All you need is a contrasting color from what the students use for their work to make your written feedback stand out. In my graduate classes of "research," I once tried using a green pen instead of red. At the end of the semester, students told me they were more motivated to rewrite because the green signaled "keep going" to them. The red made them feel their work was all wrong. "Stop. Don't bother." I have invested in many green pens ever since. I have shared this technique with numerous teacher friends, and those who have adopted this same approach indicated a difference in the motivation of their students' willingness to rewrite.

Make sure students have enough PRACTICE time in school to learn new skills.

Do not rely on the home environment to stimulate students to do their best work. Some students do not even have a table on which to work, nor an environment conducive to learning at home. The time and opportunity for assistance that you provide in school may be the only chance a student has to practice skills.

Help students learn from their mistakes.

When I was in graduate school, I approached a professor to discuss some items he marked wrong on a test. He immediately became defensive. I got the impression he thought I was there to complain about his evaluation. In fact, I knew what was wrong. I just did not know *why*. He altered his demeanor when I made it clear that I really wanted to learn the correct processes for what I had erred on in the test. For the most part, students really do want to know how they could correct their mistakes in testing. Take the time not merely to show students their mistakes, but also to point out corrective measures. Sometimes students need to know what is wrong as well as *why* it is wrong.

When students incorrectly answer a question, pose another question to redirect them.

This is easier said than done. Take time to THINK for yourself. Remember, you want to provide an environment where students can learn. So, turn an incorrect response into another question to motivate students to think further, to continue to respond to questioning. This strategy of questioning is stressful for students to begin with, so accept all responses. Just divert those students in error to think in another direction.

Create an environment where students feel comfortable asking questions.

Give positive feedback to students. Do not yell at them! No question is a "dumb" question, nor are there "stupid" questions. How many times has one of your students started with "This may be a dumb question, but . . ."? There is something wrong if we allow students to think this way. If students are to learn, they need to be encouraged to ask questions. Besides, I always tell my students that if one person has a question, chances are several other students have the same question but do not want to ask.

Mistakes are okay.

When you ask students to do something they seem unsure about, if your attitude is "anything's okay" as long as an attempt is made, then students will be more apt to take a stab at the task. Continue to ask students to work at a new task, and encourage students to "try."

Make purposeful mistakes.

Once in a while, make a purposeful mistake. See if students recognize it and if not, point it out to them. Sometimes I will share an "untruth" with my students. They get so used to "listening" that they do not really "hear." Sometimes I will have to point out the untruth, which makes them pay more attention and motivates them to find further errors. This keeps them on their toes . . . for a little while anyway.

Make sure testing is NOT the top priority.

Refrain from teaching "content" and instead teach strategies for learning so that, ultimately, students will test well. (The ACT sponsors local workshops that teach success strategies.) Success in the Miller Analogy

Test depends on recognizing relationships, not merely knowing vocabulary. Teach skills and strategies for testing, rather than merely facts and information which students can simply find in the text, a reference book, or on the Internet.

Admit your unintentional mistakes.

Do not cover up your mistakes. Admit your mistake and try to correct it while pointing out to students that it is *okay* to make mistakes. If you do not know something, admit it. Teachers cannot be walking encyclopedias. Teach students to locate and gather information, and you do the same. So, if you admit that you do not know something, find out. Then share your information with students.

Encourage students to participate.

Point out to students that in industry, teamwork is important. In school, the class members make up a team. Each person contributes to the achievement of a goal. Stress that success in business depends on participation, as does success in school.

POSITIVE FEEDBACK IS NECESSARY

For students to develop the mindset that they can learn, they can accomplish tasks, they can do well, students need positive feedback for who they are and what they can do. Teachers need to recognize the positive aspects of students. Try some of the following strategies to address this issue.

Write encouraging notes.

This takes time, but you will find that students will recognize your interest in their learning. Encourage students to continue to work with comments like "good start," "keep going," "nice try, continue to work with this."

Verbally tell students "good job" or "nice try."

We can write all the positive comments we want to on student work, but every once in a while students really need to "hear" us tell them they have done well, especially when other students are able to overhear these positive comments. Seize the opportunity to verbally tell students when they have done something well.

Point out correct answers and "good" work as well as errors to fix.

Teachers find it easy to point out mistakes. It takes time to point out what is good or acceptable. I have had so many students thank me for letting them know what they are doing "right." It is so easy for us to point out student mistakes, but we also need to recognize what students do right to encourage them to build on the strengths they possess. Ever had a student look at the mistakes and then ask if there was "anything right"? I have. Try to balance your feedback with positive phrases along with constructive comments for fixing mistakes.

Always recognize a job well done.

Point out strengths that your students exhibit. (So, what made it so good?) Even students who regularly get top grades appreciate knowing what strengths they possess or demonstrate that earn them those top grades. Let students know when they have expressed themselves well in critically thinking about an issue, organizing their thoughts into a well-constructed essay, and so on.

Use stickers.

All students like stickers! (Stickers are NOT just for elementary students!) I put a smiley face sticker on the bottom of the third page of a semester exam for my college students once, and their anxiety over the test itself was visibly reduced. I have put seasonal stickers on students' work when they have least expected it and turned apprehension and discouragement into smiles. I have put scratch-and-sniff stickers on a page of directions for a complex project and found students to be more interested to get started on the task. I have observed the disappointment on the faces of adults who did not find a Halloween sticker on their work-out record sheets at the gym when a worker simply overlooked their record sheets while applying stickers to the records of others. I have also heard criticism for using stickers. In my experience, the use of stickers affects students in positive ways. I continue to use them.

Utilize schedules of reinforcement.

Slavin (1997) offers a behavioral approach to motivating students which includes the use of schedules of reinforcement. This refers to the frequency with which reinforcement is provided for a student, or the amount of time which passes between episodes of reinforcement. This is an aspect of behavioral theories that really does merit the attention of teachers. As human beings, we all need a pat on the back once in a while. The same goes for our students. Some students need this reinforcement more often than others. We need to figure out how often each student needs reinforcement, and try to provide it on a schedule that works for that student. Use reinforcement on a schedule that is necessary for each student. Some students need constant reinforcement. So, provide it all the time. This is continuous reinforcement. Two major schedules are ratio and interval. Ratio refers to the number of behaviors that must take place before reinforcement occurs. For instance, for every five completed homework assignments submitted, the student might receive a coupon which has value for the student. Interval reinforcement takes place after a period of time. For instance, reinforcement can occur at any particular time during the process of creating a major project.

Use informal conferencing with students to communicate positive things.

Occasionally, I hold a "conference" with an individual student about the strengths and positive characteristics a student has been exhibiting. This conference usually begins because a student has approached me about a different matter and I capitalize on this event by sharing comments about positive behaviors with that student. The same is true when I have small groups of students working on a task. Our communication begins with comments about the task. But again, I take advantage of the situation by extending the focus to other positive characteristics I had been observing. Students are pleased and sometimes surprised by my comments. This approach can help students maintain or increase their motivational levels to continue to work and do well.

Let students know when the goal is achieved.

Effective teachers take larger, long-range goals and break those into smaller, short-term achievable ones. What we need to do is communicate with students about those short-term goals and let students know when these are achieved. All too often we fail to tell students when they have reached a short-term goal. We tend to move on, taking students to the next rung on the ladder without ensuring that students know what is happening. Students need to have the satisfaction of reaching one goal before striving toward another. Teachers simply need to tell students when they have reached that point and are moving toward the next targeted goal.

Be sincere. Mean what you say.

Talk to students as fellow citizens. Converse with them as people, people who just happen to be younger. Smile when you are pleased. Frown when you are not. Show a concerned look when it is necessary. Be sincere. Students know when you say one thing but mean another. Mean what you say and make sure your facial and bodily gestures are in sync with each other.

For every negative comment, make two positive ones.

As educators we would like to make "constructive" comments to students rather than "negative" ones. However, once in a while our intended constructive comments are construed as negative by students. Therefore, make it a goal for yourself to make two positive comments for every constructive one to help students maintain a level of self-esteem that will encourage them to keep trying.

Find some way to compliment all students.

Sometimes a positive comment about something personal rather than schoolwork sends a message to students that you care. You noticed. A comment about a new hair style, a hair cut, or a flattering color of clothing can make students feel like they really do matter in school. Then find something the student does well, and extend the compliment to this skill or characteristic.

SELF-CONCEPT AFFECTS THE MINDSET

Students who feel good about themselves will learn and accomplish much. Teachers can provide numerous opportunities for students to increase their sense of self-esteem and further develop a positive self-concept. Consider implementing any of the following strategies that may help provide the impetus for students to do well because they feel good about themselves and have developed some level of self-confidence.

Put a motivational saying or thought for the day on the board.

There are lots of little books available for purchase at stationery, book, and gift stores with quotes or thoughts that encourage development of the character traits we desire for all citizens of our society. Put a motivational saying or thought on the board or a special place on a bulletin board. Point it out to students. Talk about it. You can use this strategy to encourage civil behavior, help students realize that others are experiencing similar difficulties in day-to-day life, look at the humorous side of living, and so on. It is your choice. Once you start using similar motivational approaches, you may wind up with a collection of little books like I have. After a few weeks of writing famous quotes on the board, I bring a book of sayings to class and allow a student to choose which to share. (Later, pass your books on to your colleagues, or trade similar resources with one another.) You might also encourage students to bring positive quotes or famous sayings to class.

Be a role model.

Be positive. Say positive things about how you view yourself. Let students know that there is something positive about every person. Students need to recognize positive characteristics about themselves and be proud of them. Share your positive qualities and characteristics with students so they know it is okay to acknowledge their own. Just tell students. It is as simple as that.

Find good things to say even when it is difficult to do so.

Take time to do this. Sometimes students challenge us in ways we would like to ignore. Find something positive to say even when it may seem difficult. I heard about a first-year teacher who was having trouble with a young man acting up in class. Mrs. C. asked the student to step into the hall for further conversation. Mrs. C. told the student that he was a leader and that however he acted in class, several other students would follow. Mrs. C. then proceeded to ask the student what kind of leader he really wanted to be. After thinking about this, the student ultimately changed his behavior. The way the teacher handled this situation was pretty insightful for a first-year teacher.

Use constructive progress reports.

Indicate to students what should be done to make progress in their learning. Then, tell students *how* they can do it. It is so easy to tell students what they are *not* doing well. Take a more constructive approach and share with students *how* they can do better. Show students they have only limitations they place on themselves. Work with students to help them recognize constructive criticism, and show them how to use it to their advantage.

Learning is lifelong. Model it. Try journaling.

Have students write. And you too! Journal writing can serve several purposes, and there are multiple references to help teachers use this strategy with students in all kinds of classes or courses. Books and articles in professional journals by teachers can give you loads of ideas to adapt journal writing to serve the needs of your students. The key here is to teach your students that journal writing can help them clarify their own thinking, serve as a stress-relief activity, and have other purposes. Model it. Write for yourself and share what journaling does for you. Write when your own students write in class. (Likewise, if you require your students to spend time reading for pleasure in class, then you do the same. You read when your students read.)

Praise in public. Criticize in private.

All teachers have heard these statements. But, sometimes we need to remind ourselves to praise publicly but criticize privately. If what we want to do as educators is help students build their own self-esteem, then we need to remember to praise them in front of their peers and save criticism for more private conversation. All too often I have found that in speaking with students privately, the student has shared something personal that clarified that student's actions. Students will share more about themselves privately than they will when their peers are within earshot. This may provide more understanding of the student's behavior. You can then act accordingly.

Show students what they do right, and help them get through learning hurdles.

When students get stuck with a task, find the stumbling block to learning. I was tutoring a middle school student in a basic math class who was having trouble subtracting three-digit numbers. I had the student orally explain to me what he was doing with the numbers as he worked through the problem. Once I figured out that the student did not understand the concept of regrouping beyond the hundreds place, I knew how to help him. I showed him what he was doing right. Then, I proceeded to talk him through his difficulty in regrouping. He was eager to do better once he knew what he was doing wrong and learned how to fix it.

Always provide feedback on assignments turned in.

If students take the TIME to do assignments, you take the TIME to read these. If you are going to assign students to do work in the first place, and students actually DO the work, then take time on your part to actually read and look at the students' work. Two situations come to mind here. The first is a colleague of mine who reads the first couple of pages of a student's work, then puts a letter grade on it based on his first impression. Consider the student who may take a few pages of writing before getting to the depth and breadth expected. Not only has my colleague missed out on what the student actually wrote, but the student has missed an opportunity for self-growth in getting appropriate feedback. The second situation is one my sister-in-law told me about. My then middle school–aged niece completed an assignment after a lengthy period of involvement. The teacher graded the completed assignment in a couple of minutes in front of my niece. Consider the deflated self-esteem of my niece, who had spent a long time to complete this assignment only to have the teacher grade it at a glance. Just a quick, positive comment on the assignment would have been welcomed. Then the teacher could have saved the evaluation itself for another time. No, teachers cannot spend as much time grading an assignment as students spend completing it. But evaluate during private time, and be sure to actually take some time to look at student work and make appropriate comments so students know you have actually taken the time to read, look at, and evaluate their work.

Write extensive comments on student work to explain a grade or their progress.

Even a student who earns an "A" wants to know what was so good about what the student did. Consider your own school experiences. How often did you get a "B" or "C" and wonder what you could have done better? Or, surprisingly, you received a "B" and wondered what was so good about it that you received that letter grade. Provide enough comments on student work that students are clear about why they earned that grade. Develop rubrics or scoring guides to help students see what exactly is expected of them in terms of their performance. Without these guides, teacher comments become even more critical.

Allow students creative choices in assignments that align with their learning styles.

Students may come up with more creative ideas than teachers for demonstrating what they know and can do. If given a choice, students will more often use their stronger skills. Visual learners might produce a PowerPoint presentation, a video, or a design poster. Audio learners might use audiotapes. Kinesthetic learners might build or construct something.

This becomes more fun for students. Learning can be fun! As a teacher, evaluating is also more engaging and fun because of the variety of assessment approaches students may have chosen.

Provide opportunities for leadership.

Remember how exciting it was in elementary school when students were allowed to help the teacher? Elementary teachers develop job charts so students take turns being a leader at accomplishing a task. Middle school and high school teachers miss the opportunities for students to develop leadership skills by neglecting to find ways for their students to be responsible for various tasks. Think about all the work needed for your environment to be effective for student learning, and then allow students to help where feasible.

Create a positive climate.

If students are exposed to a positive environment, a positive climate in your teaching and learning area, then perhaps they will be more positive in everyday life. Surround your teaching area with positive sayings, posters, and bright colors. You might elect to use the Positive Word List for a writing activity (see Resource C for this list). Have students write a paragraph using selected words, using as many words as they can; or create whatever other activities you might think of where this list of positive words might be useful. You could even challenge students to add more words to the basic list.

Involve students in decision making for themselves or the class as a whole.

As a teacher, you are not in this alone. You have a room full of students who can help you make decisions. You do not have to do everything yourself. You are a facilitator of learning. That facilitation includes providing situations where students can be a part of their own learning. This includes decision making. From room arrangements to rules of behavior to assessment strategies, and even *teaching*, students can help make decisions! Let them!

Make sure students have had enough practice before being evaluated.

Assessing what students know and can do should be fair and accurate. Make sure students have had enough time to practice and acquire competence before they are evaluated.

Use formative evaluation frequently before utilizing summative evaluations.

Find student weaknesses. Identify elements needing clarification either in your teaching or in student learning. Use oral or written assessments. Frequent formative evaluation will help identify these elements. Take the time to find out if your students are really learning and practicing what they should.

Use student input.

Having a say in what is taught, and how, provides an opportunity for self-growth. Students should be included in limited curricular decisions at the middle and high school levels. Students are sometimes neglected when it comes to curricular decisions, yet they have the most to gain. One year when I was teaching a basic health class with high school students, I took a risk with the order of unit topics to be covered over the semester. We had about 10 separate units. When I studied the topics, it really did not matter which one preceded another. So I took it to the students. I wrote each unit topic on the board. Then, I proceeded to discuss each topic and some activities I envisioned for each. I asked students to vote on the sequence in which we would study the units. I had a student lead the voting. I made copies for the students of their final order of topics they would study. It was a fun semester! What better way to provide opportunities for self-growth, an increase in self-esteem, and enhancement of a positive self-concept than to have input into your own learning and that of your peers? You might also be sure there is student representation on curricular committees. Their insight can be valuable!

SUMMARY

Teachers can affect the mindset of students with the strategies selected for teaching and the environment provided for learning. If students believe they can succeed, in all probability, they will. Educators need to recognize that all students can learn, though in varying degrees. Students learn from making mistakes and being able to correct those mistakes. But, teachers need to provide the environment that makes students feel that it is okay to make mistakes in the first place. In addition, students need positive feedback for what they do. Students need to know they have the qualities, strengths, and characteristics needed to succeed. Sometimes students do not know they have these unless we tell them. Hopefully, all this leads students to self-growth and the ultimate development of a mindset reflective of increased self-esteem and positive self-concept.

2 Motivation Is Influenced Through Observation

No printed word
Nor spoken plea
Can teach young minds
What they should be

Not all the books
On all the shelves
But what the teachers
Are themselves

—Anonymous

S tudents watch what teachers do and how teachers act. Students learn through our example. If Bandura's (1977) theory of observational learning could be applied between teachers and students as well as from student to student, we might be able to say with some conviction that if we exhibit the characteristics that reflect positive, motivated happiness, because of who we are and what we do as teachers, then our students might find the desire to be positive, motivated, and happy students. Students might be excited about school and motivated to learn.

I heard Neila Connors (a nationally known educator with the Middle School movement and owner of Positive Connections) once say that "you can't burn out if you've never been on fire." Students watch what we do and how we act, then learn through our example. I have a handout in my files from Neila Connors (Connors, 1990) in which she referenced the St. Louis Park (MN) School District as having published a newsletter for their teachers and all employees which listed characteristics of "non-burned out professionals." Among these were the following:

- They have a sense of accomplishment and self-worth which is reflected mainly in attitude.
- They feel there is a purpose in life, particularly their own.
- They enjoy their job and look forward to going to work.
- They have good perspective on their personal, professional, and social life.
- They are capable of laughing at themselves.
- They are willing to consider alternatives and change, and are able to handle change. (as cited in Connors, 1990)

Students watch their teachers. If we cannot be excited about teaching and learning, then we cannot expect the students to be excited. It is as simple as that.

One of the most challenging tasks for students during the adolescent years is in dealing with peer pressure. Teachers can help students learn what it takes to be happy, self-confident, strong individuals by example. Teach students how to offset peer pressure by demonstrating how we avoid succumbing to our own adult peer pressure.

PROJECT INTENSITY AND ENTHUSIASM

Always remember that students continually watch their teachers. If teachers project intensity and enthusiasm for their role in the learning process, then students stand a better chance to also become excited, and thereby motivated, to learn. Consider the following suggestions.

Leave your personal problems at home.

Given life and all its experiences, some days can seem more up or more down physically, mentally, emotionally, or psychologically. Students need you at your best. Be real, but do not saddle students with your problems. They have enough of their own. I have overheard teachers tell students about the trials and tribulations that teachers were experiencing with other teachers, administrators, and even the teachers' own families. Students do not need this. Forget your own difficulties and try to focus on your students. They can certainly empathize with you on major life challenges, but students do not need to be a part of your everyday problems. Students need you at your best!

Wear a smile.

Smiles, like yawns, are contagious. See what happens when you smile at your students, especially early in the school year while students are still trying to get acquainted with you. I had many college students over the years who indicated on my teaching evaluations that they knew they would survive my class in "Research Methods" because I came into class the first night smiling. In all the years I spent with adolescents, I tried to put on a smile when students came into the classroom and when I was ready to begin a lesson. It does make a difference in the attitudes of students.

Laugh.

Laugh at yourself, especially when you make a mistake. What? You never err in class? Ha! Reflect again! Ever watch the bloopers and blunders on television and laugh when people make mistakes? So, be human and laugh, and your students will laugh with you. I cannot tell you how many times over the years I have rattled on in class only to catch myself and then said to my students, "That did not make much sense, did it?" If they have not been paying attention up to that point, my admission brings them back to the lesson!

Foster student-teacher interaction.

Students are more motivated when the teacher involves them in the class. Remember that you, as a teacher, are a facilitator of learning. As such, you should be providing an environment in which students can learn. Lecturing helps only the audio-learner. *You* become the focal point of the lecture. *You* have already been to school. *You* have already learned. Try to change the focus of the lesson toward students. Involve *students*. Get *students* to talk to you and to each other. Capitalize on the desire of *students* to talk. Just focus that talk in the direction of the lesson and its objectives.

Come to class dressed appropriately for the lesson.

Outward appearance is important. Like what you do and who you are. Take time to project that you are a professional. Students will notice. Students observe the differences in behaviors of others based on physical appearance. (Note how student behavior is affected on "picture day.") Show students you care by taking the time to dress appropriately and professionally. On the other hand, join in with students and alter your dress for "special" days that call for unity such as everyone wearing jeans, school T-shirts, pajamas, and so on.

Be ACTIVE . . . even if you are not enthusiastic.

Even teachers cannot be enthusiastic about everything they teach. I have never been a fan of the sport of basketball. But, in teaching the game and its skills and strategies, I maintained an active attitude by discussing local athletes and teams with my students. I worked hard to show my students how exciting the sport could be. I do not think my students ever realized that basketball was not my personal sport of choice either as an athlete or teacher. Students deserve the opportunity to develop their own interests, not merely adopt yours.

Keep visual contact.

Maintain the attention and interest of students by getting out of the "T" zone. In the typical classroom, a teacher tends to "eyeball" students down the middle and across the back rows, the "T" zone. Check yourself on this one. Have a colleague visit your class and provide feedback for you on where you tend to focus among students. Or better yet, videotape yourself. Make an effort to look at each of your students. Nothing gets or maintains their attention more than direct eye contact.

Add VARIETY to your voice and expression.

Videotape yourself, and look at what the students see. Find out if your voice and mannerisms attempt to maintain the interest of the students during the lesson. I did not realize how "dictatorial" my voice projected until I heard myself talking on a videotape. Oh, I moved around the room and was fairly animated in my gestures, but my voice was a turnoff. I have learned to soften it and project a warmer tone.

Use one-on-one interaction.

Encourage personal communication with students. All too often there are so many students in our classes that there are several students we never really get to know very well—who they are, how they learn. An easy way to encourage students to communicate with you is to, on occasion, distribute a 3″ × 5″ card, a memo sheet, or the like and ask students to respond to a particular prompt. I like to use 3″ × 5″ cards because they are inexpensive and easy to handle. Ask students to respond to questions like: "How are you doing with your project?" "How do you feel about the issues we talked about today?" Remind students to explain the reasons for what they write. You cannot always talk with each student on a daily basis, but you *can* communicate! You need to realize, though, that effective communication includes feedback. So, be sure to read what students write and provide enough comment that students know you have paid attention to what they wrote. Comment directly on the student cards. Then give them back to the students. Be careful you do not "judge" what students write; just acknowledge their communication.

Have a positive attitude about what you are teaching.

Enjoy what you are teaching, and know why you are teaching it. Students watch what you do. If you are a teacher of mathematics and you project enthusiasm for all the implications of mathematics in everyday life, then perhaps students will find it relevant to put more effort into their study of mathematics. If you want students to be excited about learning in your content area, then *you* have to be excited and positive about what you teach.

Act out content.

Show AND tell. Provide a visual picture. Only a small percentage of your students are audio-learners. Many more students will remember what you say if you also show them. Adding gestures or acting out a scenario relative to a topic will maintain the interest of students and perhaps add some clarity for learning.

Be prepared.

Knowing what you are doing and being organized and prepared to teach sends a message to students that they are important to you. Put an outline on the board for the lesson. Have handouts and other materials ready. Be sure that media and technology to be used is operating effectively before class begins. Students care when they observe that you have taken the time to get ready to teach and help them learn.

Acquire an attitude of ENERGY.

Try new things. Seek to utilize a variety of strategies. Be excited about student learning. Talk to other teachers about what works for them and adopt what may be applicable to you and your students. Attend professional development workshops and conferences to glean new ideas. Surround yourself with positive people who exhibit energy!

Come to class with a happy frame of mind.

Point out things in daily life to be happy about. There is a book called *14,000 Things to Be Happy About* by Barbara Kipfer (1990). Each day, you might want to write out one or more of these things on the board. If students cannot relate to one, maybe they will be able to relate to another. Or, select a student to make three choices to share with the class. If nothing else, read an item or two for yourself. The point is: There are so many things in life to be happy about! Recognizing this will help students develop more positive attitudes toward life and learning. If students see you happy, chances are they will be, too.

Greet students at the door.

Let students know you recognize they are there. Say something personal to students as they come into class. Call students by name. When I am initially learning students' names at the beginning of the year, I ask students to help me by telling me their names when we pass each other on the stairs or in the hallways. I find that students continue to do this long after I recognize them! They seem to take delight in beating me to the punch by telling me who they are before I can state their names. If I am in my classroom, I try to say hello to students, by name, as they enter. They know I recognize they are there!

Move around the classroom.

Get out of the zone. Just as teachers tend to look mostly at students in the "T" zone, teachers also tend to walk the same paths in the classroom over and over again. Take a different route. Move down a different aisle, walk around the tables or desks you tend to ignore, and teach from the back of the room or on the side once in a while. Be intense about what you are teaching, no matter where you are in the learning environment!

Every once in a while, do something unusual or unexpected.

Create an environment that is a pleasant surprise. It is motivating to be in an environment of the unexpected or the unknown. When I used an audiotape for a lesson on teaching from the heart (Purkey, 1990), William Purkey, who was the speaker, mentioned having fresh flowers in the classroom, so I made sure to have a bouquet of fresh flowers in the classroom. He said a classroom should be an inviting and pleasant place to be. My students were pleasantly surprised to see fresh flowers on the table at the front of the room. At the end of the lesson, I even gave one flower from the bouquet to each student in that class as each exited the classroom. You must know those students remembered that lesson!

Create an interesting/energetic/motivational room environment.

Ask yourself if your classroom is an exciting place to be. If the appearance of your room or the environment in which you teach is other than welcoming, inviting, exciting, then do something about it! If you do not like the atmosphere, imagine the attitude of your students. Change or alter what you can to make the environment a nice place to be. Put colorful posters with positive messages or interesting pictures on your walls and bulletin boards. Create an atmosphere that projects intensity and enthusiasm for learning and living.

MODEL SELF-CONFIDENCE

Because students watch what educators do and how they react to various situations, teachers must always be aware that they are setting an example of appropriate behavior. Peer pressure exists with teachers as well as with students. It is important to model for students how to offset peer pressure by being happy, self-confident individuals. This can be done in many ways.

React in mature ways.

Be aware of how you react to situations like interruptions during the lesson. Students watch what you do. Sometimes our displeased facial expressions during an unexpected announcement via the public address system or a visitor at the classroom door send a negative message to students. Be flexible with interruptions or unexpected occurrences and learn to "go with the flow." If students see that you are not rattled by the unexpected, but can accommodate the disruption calmly and easily return to the lesson, they will learn how to respond to unexpected situations that interrupt their own life activities. A colleague reminded me about teachers who express displeasure at the mention of our statewide testing program. My colleague told a group to teachers that when they express this negativism in terms of rolling their eyes or frowning about the program while they are in the company of students, these teachers send a message to students that the test is not important. When students get this message, it is no wonder some of them do not try their best when taking the test. So, be cognizant of how you act or react in front of students.

Invite professional visitors to your class.

You are not in this alone. Students see you all the time. Invite other professional adults to come to your class to help demonstrate positive, confident behaviors. The topic is not important, just a demonstrated behavior of a happy, confident adult is what is important. Invite a counselor from your school, the local DARE officer, or some other professional, positive, and active person from your community to visit your classes.

Share with students what you have done, are doing, or have experienced in the past.

Use situations similar to those encountered by your students like losing a loved one, conflict with a friend, and other life encounters and share your insights regarding your experiences. Teach students coping skills that can help them work through their own experiences. When my father died, my students wanted to know what happened. I talked about it. I answered their questions. Life presents situations to which students and teachers can all relate.

Share "motivational" efforts with your own colleagues and, when appropriate, with your students.

Start with your own colleagues and share your strategies for maintaining the motivation to not just teach and teach well, but to live a happy, contented life. Just recently one of my colleagues approached me with a dejected attitude toward his job. It was not the teaching he was concerned with, but attending meetings and dealing with his self-centered colleagues that was getting him down. I shared with him some strategies that work for me, such as giving myself permission to take time to read a novel and not feel guilty because I might feel I should be grading papers. I examined my time management and made some adjustments so I did not spend half my weekends on schoolwork. I surround myself with a workspace that includes a tabletop waterfall, a scented candle, and soft, soothing music. I also plan ahead to take tasks that are not fully mind-consuming to meetings with me so that I can accomplish my own tasks, yet still pay attention and participate. We have a responsibility to help motivate each other.

When it is appropriate, I also share these self-motivational strategies with my students.

Give examples of personal work . . . like a poem of your own.

I have shared my own personal work with students on multiple occasions. I still have a leaf collection I put together in high school that I bring to class to demonstrate organizational skills and pride in my own accomplishment. I have also shared professional research I initiated, articles I have had published, and what I have learned both personally and professionally. Students need to observe the pride and sense of accomplishment that you have in yourself.

Follow instructions from superiors.

Students watch what teachers do, and for some reason are especially interested in what we say to one another. When we are requested to follow instructions from superiors, whether we agree with those instructions or not, we need to demonstrate to students that there is a hierarchy in life situations that dictates appropriate civil behaviors. Students will learn by watching how we react and what we do.

Be strong. Stand your ground.

Our society has a foundation in several freedoms. One of those is freedom of speech. There are occasions when we need to take a stand and not succumb to pressures to act in ways that conflict with what we believe. A specific example might be a discussion of adopting assertive discipline as a management approach in a school. We need to speak up in support of or in disagreement with this approach. Consideration for adopting or eliminating corporal punishment in a school is another example. In appropriate situations we need to share these conversations with students to help them learn that life presents occasions that call for us to be strong and confident and stand up for what we believe.

Show general interest in subject matter.

Regardless of the "content" or subject specialties of teachers, there is always a topic we are excited to teach as well as one or more topics that we do not look forward to covering. That is okay. Life does not always present us with circumstances we appreciate to the same degree. So, teach all topics with at least a general interest. Show students with your attitudes that it is okay to have different degrees of interest. But remember, if you are not interested and excited about what you are teaching, then how can you expect students to be interested and excited about learning?

Relate to students positive ways to deal with peer pressure.

Sometimes students experience peer pressure to do things they do not really want to do. Acknowledge to students that you realize this happens. Then, share your own experiences of peer pressure at an adult level, where you have made your own decisions to act, rather than be pressured to do something you wanted to avoid. An example might be when teachers attend professional conferences while their colleagues spend the time with friends either shopping or sightseeing. The latter activities are okay as long as the school district is not providing financial support for attending the conference. I have seen teachers leave meetings early to attend social affairs because their colleagues pressured them to do so. This happens locally as well as at state and national conferences. Share similar experiences of when you had to do what you knew was right for you, in spite of peer pressure to do otherwise. Keep this age-appropriate. What and how much you share with younger adolescents will certainly be different than what you share with older adolescents. The important thing is to share positive ways to deal with peer pressure.

SUMMARY

Motivation is influenced through observation. Students watch what we do and how we react in various situations. We are models to our students, and it would behoove us to remain cognizant of this. Students watch what we do in school as well as observe us and how we act. If we want students to be excited about learning, then we have to be excited about teaching. If we want students to become strong, healthy, self-confident individuals, then we have to show them how to do this in spite of, or perhaps because of, the peer pressure they experience during adolescence. Peer pressure is experienced by adults as well as adolescents, who sometimes feel they are the only ones who have to deal with this. If teachers can share appropriate situations with students where teachers are personally successful in overcoming peer pressure, then modeling by example is positive. Students observe their teachers and are influenced by their behaviors. Projecting enthusiasm for learning and modeling self-confidence are critical for student excitement and interest.

3 Motivation Is Affected by Timing

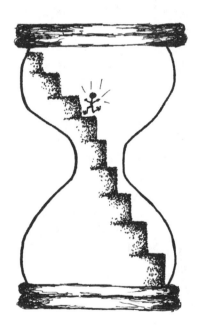

Maslow theorizes that basic human needs operate in a hierarchical manner. This means that lower level needs must be met before the individual may be motivated to pursue needs at a higher level.

—Maslow (1954)

The basic issue is timing . . . *when* it is that a student is ready for learning, or needs something that teachers can provide in order for the student to be more motivated to learn. Maslow's (1954) hierarchy of needs begins with the foundation of satisfying one's basic physiological needs, then proceeds to the satisfaction of needs related to safety, followed by those of love and belonging, and ultimately capped by needs related to self-esteem, then self-actualization. In keeping with the spirit of Maslow's hierarchy, teachers must first be sure that a student's physiological needs are met before a student's needs for safety (being free from harm and having shelter) and love and belonging can be addressed. Only if all previous needs are met can teachers help students meet their needs for self-esteem (being respected and viewed as competent), and only then can we even contemplate providing an environment in which students can experience a sense of self-actualization. Maslow (1968) indicates that fewer than 5% of the population would achieve this level of having fulfilled one's potential and being at peace with oneself and the universe. Therefore, the timing for motivational intervention is affected by a student's level of need. *When* to provide stimuli that might affect a student's motivational level is critical to learning. Teachers are further challenged by the fact that a student's needs can fluctuate from one level to the next, seemingly up and down a staircase within any given period of time.

So, based on the concept of timing and the issue of student needs, educators can do two main things. First, teachers can recognize and plan for the fact that the entry level of students in any given class varies in terms of timing with regard to their interests, abilities, and especially their needs. Second, teachers can provide appropriate objectives to meet students' needs at any given time.

TIMING OF NEEDS VARIES

It is important for educators to recognize that students who come into their classes do so representing a variety of interests and abilities. Additionally, those same students have a wide range of needs which must be met to help maximize the motivation to learn. The challenge for educators is to satisfy students' needs on a schedule which coincides with the need of any given student. Teachers can use numerous strategies to address these issues and challenges.

Provide or support breakfast programs, early lunch time, and snack opportunities.

Maslow's hierarchy of needs has as its foundation the theory that the physiological needs of a person must be met before any other needs.

Teachers need to support any opportunities that schools present in meeting these basic needs of students. Sometimes all that is necessary is for teachers to give verbal support for these programs. Other times, teachers may need to volunteer time to maintain a program. In some cases, it might require a teacher's initiation for a program to even get off the ground. At the very least, teachers can provide snack opportunities for students within the classroom, especially early in the school day and at midmorning. Teachers who feel their students might benefit from having additional snacks available could, after consultation with their principal, pursue one of the following:

1. Contact the food service director for the district to discuss possible alternatives for providing additional snacks.

2. Discuss the issue with parent volunteers for their involvement in addressing the issue. (They could assist with either providing snack items or money to support the purchase of these items.)

3. Contact local grocers in an effort to partner with the school in donating occasional snack or fruit items for students.

4. Provide occasional snack items yourself.

Schedule hands-on activities, especially in classes during early morning and right after lunch.

Some students are not necessarily "morning" people, and scheduling hands-on activities early will help those students become more engaged in the learning process. Likewise, right after lunch, the "morning" student will begin to feel a lag, and incorporating hands-on activities after lunch will help those students remain active. Recognize physiological differences between your students.

Provide or support before- and afterschool programs (latchkey).

Society in the United States in the 21st century has more parents working outside the home than ever before. More and more students are left to fend for themselves when they return home after school. Safety and security are important issues with students. Motivated students will accept responsibility to accomplish school tasks on their own. Other students, however, need someone to provide the guidance and encouragement to study and practice the skills they learned in class that day. Effective and dedicated teachers will work together in a school to provide time before and after school for students who need adult supervision or encouragement for learning. In times of financial crises, school districts will not be able to compensate teachers for their extra time in school. But teacher volunteers and assistance from other available adults, like grandparents, can help these programs succeed.

Get to know students' changing needs. Care!

I have heard it said so often by educators that students do not care how much you know, they only know how much you care. Students need a secure environment in which to thrive. Sometimes students need to be left alone. Sometimes students need to be acknowledged. Sometimes students just need to be given a "break." Teachers need to be aware of the changes in students' needs so those needs can be met. This demands that teachers pay attention to students, not just the subject, because a student may not usually need much attention, but a changing event in that student's life may alter that need. A close relative who is gravely ill, an unexpected accident in the family, or unpleasant confrontations between family members can influence an abrupt change in the needs of a student.

Reassess.

How secure are students in the content area or the subject you are teaching? How ready are they to learn what you are about to teach? Find out what students already know and can do by preassessing their abilities before you begin to teach. Try conducting a simple survey, either orally or in writing, relevant to the content information students are about to learn. Find out not just what they already know about the subject, but also their attitudes and opinions toward the topic. This should give you more insight into the motivational levels of students toward learning during the next instructional unit. You can then adjust your instructional strategies accordingly.

Communicate relevance.

So often we hear students ask teachers how or what the current lesson has to do with anything. Students need to know how the topic relates to them. The key here is helping students understand the relevance of school to their lives right now, not 5 to 10 years from now. Security in knowing how something affects them is important to students. Students are not motivated to learn when teachers tell them that what they are studying will be useful to them "someday." Remember the age of your students and make connections for them between what they are learning and their present lives.

Present to students information on which they have a knowledge base.

Sometimes students feel insecure in a class because they do not know enough. Teachers unconsciously put students in this position by forcing students to participate in discussions on topics for which students have no basic knowledge. Help students feel more secure in your class and more willing to express their thoughts and ideas by making sure students have had the time and opportunity to develop a broad enough knowledge base on the given topic.

Provide time.

The school day is only so long, but teachers need to make a conscious effort to provide time in school for students to learn. Often teachers get caught up in using the class period for conveying information to students rather than providing enough time for students to learn. Teachers can make it a habit to plan for time during each lesson for students to reinforce what is to be learned or to engage in other activities that can provide more depth and breadth on the topic. In any case, teachers must provide time in class for study and independent practice, because for some students that is the only time in the day they will have for learning. Security is enhanced when students have had sufficient time to practice what they need to know. Assuming students learned in school and will have time to practice at home is overly optimistic.

Pick your battles.

Sometimes when students feel insecure or when their sense of belonging is threatened, students will behave in ways that are inappropriate for maximum learning. Do not make a big deal out of little things. Teachers need to recognize these behaviors for what they are: attention-getting. Many times, a little individual attention will alleviate student insecurities. Teachers can then avoid calling the attention of the entire class to one student's misbehavior, thereby disrupting the learning process.

Find out student likes, dislikes, and interests. Relate class activities to what you find out. Get to know your students.

It goes without saying that not all the students in your classes will be interested in the subject area you are trying to teach. If you find out what your students like and are interested in, you can use that information to connect with concepts and information from the subject you are teaching.

This will increase a student's sense of belonging. Make a template and simply ask students to list their likes, dislikes, and interests, then work to make connections to the subject area for students. Or, you can ask students to simply write you a letter in class, sharing their likes, dislikes, and outside interests. Read these letters later when you have time to focus on what students are telling you. I have made it a practice to have each student write me a letter at the beginning of the year. I tell students what kind of information I need to know. I ask students to tell me basic demographic information (where they have lived, how many other children are in the family, their own birth order within the family). I ask students to tell me a little about their schooling (where they have gone to school, the subject areas they really like and why, the subject areas they find challenging and why). Then, I ask students to write about what they hope to get out of the class they have with me. I read these letters immediately to get a little insight into who my students are. Then, I save and reread them often through the year to remind myself what students have said.

Be nondiscriminatory.

It is easy to help students learn when they are already active and interested in the subject. However, we need to recognize that all students need to learn. Teachers need to make a special effort to spend time with each student. It might help to target several students each day so that by the end of a school week, you have made an effort to work with, talk to, or otherwise recognize each student at some time during the week. Check your class rosters at midweek to note which students you still need to recognize by the end of the day on Friday. Love and belonging are essential for students.

Plan activities according to the season or time of the year.

Face it; those of us who live in a varied seasonal climate react to seasonal changes in various ways. Even if you ignore "seasonal" changes in climate, the fact of living through the passing of a New Year (a stretch of time away from formal schooling), holidays like Labor Day, and celebrations like birthdays provides opportunities for connecting learning to the natural cycle of life and increasing a sense of belonging. Therefore, integrate activities in schools and your classes that recognize and coincide with these influencing periods in students' lives.

Plan according to current and political events.

Incorporate current events into your lessons, or at least connect these events to students' lives. Students need to feel the sense of belonging to a society. They need to feel that what they do as citizens can make a difference.

(Incidentally, voting rates among young citizens continue to be low.) If students can learn early in their school years that they really belong, maybe teachers can influence them enough to make a positive change in our country's future through active involvement and participation. Local, state, and national elections, along with issues of concern at each government level, provide fuel for further discussions and activities.

Recognize student effort.

All of us need positive reinforcement at one time or another. Teachers need to remember that some students need recognition for their efforts all the time while other students can remain motivated with a little encouragement every once in a while. A sense of love and belonging can be satisfied when students are recognized for their efforts to succeed and are encouraged to do their optimal best. Tell students as often as needed when they are progressing toward expected goals.

Use positive scoring.

Look for correct and accurate work. Comment on the positive. Calculate what the student has done that is right. So often teachers evaluate and score student work by looking for and evaluating *errors* and indicating how many points are being taken off the positive score. Think the opposite. Students get discouraged when they see a number of errors. Indicate how many points the student has earned. Write "+25/30" rather than "−5." Help students increase self-esteem by highlighting their successes.

Take student opinions seriously.

If students express opinions, it is because they have something pressing on their minds. Students need to know they play an important role in their own learning and that their input is important. Ignoring students or not responding to them affects their self-esteem. I have heard students criticize their teachers, stating that teachers do not listen to them. Sometimes teachers listen to what students have to say, but delay responding to a later time, or maybe never. Students need immediate feedback. Take the opinions and ideas from students seriously. Let them know you do by your quick and sincere response. What students may have to say may not be important to you, but it is important and relevant to them.

Give students decision-making power.

Students can develop a better sense of self-esteem when given some decision-making power. As a teacher, you do not have to make all the rules, nor decide on the guidelines for an assignment. Once in a while, let students help make decisions. Teachers can provide guidance, but students should be allowed input into their own learning.

Allow students to provide input for future work.

To help students who are less motivated become aware of the future, share your rationale for units of study and ask students to provide suggestions for how learning goals can be achieved. You can do this by asking students to brainstorm ideas in small groups or in a larger class discussion. Then, help students develop a more secure sense of self-esteem by following up and by listening to student suggestions and incorporating their ideas into future projects and assignments.

Help students write goals for themselves.

If teachers are to help move students to a secure level of self-esteem, then teachers need to incorporate strategies that will help students clarify their own values and goals. I did this with middle-level students by teaching them how to write goals for themselves for specific instructional units. Students were to think about what they wanted to achieve by the end of the unit and then write it down. (I limited students to no more than three goals.) I then asked students to think about what they could do each day of one week toward achieving these goals. I taught students to write their objectives in measurable terms so they could assess their own progress as time went on. Yes, this took more class time, but I think the end result of students learning more about themselves and what it takes for their own success was well worth it. (See Resource D for examples you can adopt for this activity.)

Teach students how to write self-reflections.

One thing I have learned over time is that self-reflection is healthy and provides a means of self-growth. A person only has to peruse the shelves of self-help books in a bookstore to recognize the need for this activity. To help students strive toward Maslow's level of self-actualization, teachers can help students learn the process of self-reflection. Teach students how to reflect, and then give students the opportunity to maintain journals or construct portfolios that should include self-reflection. Read articles in professional journals like *Educational Leadership* or journals published by the education association affiliated with your academic content area for additional pointers in teaching students how to reflect on their own learning. Reflective writing is a frequent topic of articles published since the late 1990s.

NEEDS DRIVE OBJECTIVES

Because students' needs vary and can fluctuate depending on time of day, time of month, time of year, or even timing of circumstances, teachers need to be flexible enough to provide appropriate objectives that attempt to meet those needs at any given time. Time, itself, is a concept that some students have difficulty comprehending. Therefore, teachers need to construct objectives in ways that allow for flexibility in the conditions and criteria for acceptable work from students and that also help students learn to manage the concept of time. Teachers might consider implementing one or more of the suggested strategies.

Create syllabi, rubrics, scoring guides, or assignment calendars so students know what is expected of them.

All too often teachers tell students *what* to do and *when* to do it, yet fail to tell students *why* they are learning something and *how they will be evaluated* on what they do. This failure to clarify for students why they are learning about a specific topic and how they will be evaluated influences student learning. Share course syllabi with students so they know the rationale, objectives, and expectations for the unit. Provide rubrics and scoring guides, or better yet, have students help design them so students know exactly what is expected and how they will be evaluated. Share a calendar of events related to the unit so students have a sense of the timeliness of activities within the unit.

Provide students with an idea of how much time may be required for each assignment.

Students will always feel a better sense of security when they know what it is that teachers expect. One of the related issues here is knowing how long, in terms of time, it may take to accomplish a task. We often tell students what to do and how to do it. But we sometimes neglect to give students an approximate period of time they will need to do the assignment. Tell students if a task will only take a "few minutes," "a little time each night for a few days," or "a lot of time." Provide guidelines for students so they can plan time for successful execution.

Provide appropriate due dates for assignments so students remember and learn time management.

Only your highly motivated students are able to accomplish tasks in timely ways on their own. The majority of your students need help. Provide due dates for all assignments, and help students remember these by giving students continual reminders. Security is increased when students learn to manage their responsibilities within a specific time frame.

Allow students to help set deadlines for their work.

Allowing students to have some input on deadlines may increase a student's sense of security and the possibility of more students accomplishing the tasks on time. My students are always more motivated to get work done when they have a chance to help decide due dates. Sometimes we have had to compromise. But, in all situations when students have had a say, there has been less moaning, groaning, and complaining and more adherence to the time constraints of given tasks. (Be reasonable and open-minded. If there is a football game on Friday night, a dance on Saturday night, and a school play, do not schedule a test for Monday morning.)

Provide reinforcement activities to students who need more time to comprehend the topic.

Some students are not ready to move forward either in terms of acquiring more information or in working or functioning at higher performance levels. These students need more time to reinforce what they already know. Provide opportunities for students to practice skills they have already learned until they feel more secure in moving forward. (While some students are doing reinforcement activities, other students can be playing roles in those reinforcement activities or doing enrichment activities on their own.)

Gradually increase the amount of information being taught.

Students are sometimes frustrated by information overload from teachers. Take time to be sure students have comprehended a basic amount of content before gradually increasing the amount during instruction. Repeat, reinforce, repeat, reinforce, and then add more to their knowledge base a little at a time as students increasingly understand what they need to know.

Use cooperative activities.

Few strategies will address a student's need for love and belonging more than that of cooperative or team activities. (Teachers need to be careful about the approach to forming teams and the inappropriate use of cooperative activities.) The main sources for information on cooperative learning are Johnson and Johnson (1994) and Slavin (1995). Many teacher-friendly books on the market provide numerous methods to successfully incorporate cooperative activities to maximize learning. Find these books at teacher bookstores as well as general bookstores located in your own community.

Constantly REVIEW to give students a feeling of accomplishment.

When students feel success and accomplishment, their level of self-esteem improves. Help students feel secure and successful by continuously reviewing important information. Remember that repetition is a form of learning. So, be patient, and repeat, review, repeat, review. (I cannot say this often enough.)

Use peer-editing groups to provide critical analysis.

When students have a chance to participate in activities where their judgment plays an important role, not only does their sense of belonging improve, but also their level of self-esteem. Students learn and can accept constructive comments sometimes more easily from their peers than from adults. Teach students the process of peer editing. Then, let them do it.

Give challenging (enrichment) assignments to students who are ready for them.

Students who already understand a given concept, have a solid knowledge base, and are able to apply past learning are ready for enriched learning experiences on a specific topic. Such experiences boost learning to a new level and ultimately enhance their sense of self-esteem. Be prepared to challenge these students with activities that will force them to further apply analysis, synthesis, and evaluation skills.

SUMMARY

Whether or not you believe in and accept Maslow's theory about a hierarchy of needs, you have to admit it gives teachers some food for thought, especially when working with adolescents. Students' interests change from day to day and sometimes several times within the same day, as do their needs. Recognize that student needs can fluctuate within any given period of time. The satisfaction of a student's needs is imperative to maximizing the student's motivation to learn. The ultimate challenge for educators is to attempt to meet the needs of students according to their timetables. Numerous strategies exist which will help educators accomplish this. Time and readiness play influential roles in a student's level of motivation to learn. Teachers need to provide appropriate objectives for students so that criteria for acceptable work from students are flexible in terms of conditions that will support students learning to manage the concept of time. Additionally, students' readiness to learn must be addressed for students to maximize their interest and motivation to accomplish what is expected of them.

4 Motivation Is Independence

Independence of thinking = New investigations

S ome students achieve success only when allowed to achieve that success at their own pace. Independence is fostered when students are allowed to make decisions for themselves and live with the consequences of those decisions. This process helps students focus on their own independent choices and assists in future decisions they may make. The social learning theory espoused by Bandura and Schunk (1981) stems from self-motivation related to goal setting and the evaluation of one's own behavior. The idea is that if a student really wants to achieve something, the student thinks that by trying hard, the student can succeed. This suggests two things: the expectation of reaching a goal, and the motivation of trying to achieve something that is of value to the student.

Educators can help students learn to make decisions by teaching them how to set goals. Sometimes students have difficulty thinking about their future aspirations, but teachers can help with this process. Encouraging student performance appraisal and providing opportunities for self-reinforcement are two ways to help foster the independence of thinking that will help lead students to new investigations. An additional suggestion for encouraging students' independence of thinking is to provide opportunities for students to role-play. Give students options for their actions so they learn to be independent in their thoughts and actions.

TEACH GOAL SETTING

I learned early in my career that students do not always know how to set educational goals. If we want students to be motivated by their own independence of thinking, then we have to begin by teaching them about setting goals and how to arrive at the objectives that will help them reach those goals. There are numerous strategies that teachers can use to help this process.

Teach students what goal setting is all about.

All too often, teachers tell students they should set goals for themselves and assume students know how to do that. An easy way to teach students about goals is to discuss issues that relate to their own lives and set up open-ended situations that force individual students to think about what the student wants to happen in the end. Specific approaches will vary with the age of your students. Young adolescents will think about goals that are more short term, whereas older adolescents can relate to goals that are more long term. The key is to have students think about something they want for themselves. Force students to write the goal(s) down. Have students list whatever it is they will have to do to reach these goals. Then, you can read these and assist those students who have difficulty with how to set appropriate goals.

Help students with self-assessment.

There are several ways you can help students focus and realize what they already know and can do on a specific topic. You can do simple activities like giving a preassessment, perhaps one based on new vocabulary words. You can try using a strategy like K-W-L (see Chapter 1) (Carr & Ogle, 1987; Ogle, 1986). You can ask students to simply write as much as they already know. I have done this with both middle school and high school students, and in almost all cases students realize they know more than they thought they did. This activity sometimes works as an initial motivating factor in that students anticipate adding to their already existing knowledge base.

Have students write their own learning goals for each instructional unit.

Once students know how to write goals for themselves, let them write goals for themselves for each instructional unit (see Resource D for examples). I did this by spending the first day of each unit introducing the concepts for the unit, then allowing students to think for themselves what they wanted to accomplish by the end of the unit. Students then wrote goals for themselves for the instructional unit followed by actions for each school day that would help them achieve their goals. (Students did self-evaluations at the end of each unit.)

Give students some input about what to teach and when.

Sometimes the topics for an instructional unit really do not have to follow a particular sequence. In cases like this, engage the students in making decisions about what to teach and what should be studied and investigated. Students might elect to study their favorite topic first, or they may decide to save the best for last. The important strategy is allowing students to have some input.

Teach students how to take notes for themselves.

There are numerous strategies that teach students how to take meaningful notes. But, what is most important is that students be allowed to write notes that are meaningful to them. Show students several strategies, then emphasize that each student must find an approach to writing notes that works for him- or herself. All the teachers I had who tried to teach note taking for research writing used the old 3″ × 5″ index card approach. That does not work for me. It took me a long time to realize that finding my own way to take notes was okay. Be flexible and help students figure out what is best for them.

Allow students to strive for self-chosen grades as a goal.

If you have not already developed a scoring guide for what is expected to achieve an "A," "B," "C," or "D" for grade reports, then now is the time to start. Students should be clear about what it takes to achieve an overall "A" or "B" grade. After allowing students time to examine the scoring guide for grade reports, have students write down the "grade" they wish to strive for. Then, ask students why they chose that goal for themselves. This information should help you assess motivational needs for individual students.

Allow students to choose activities that help reach their goals.

Allow students to choose the means by which they can meet their goals and objectives. I have had students write me poems and short stories, and one student even created a game that other students in class could play to reinforce unit concepts. Keep an open mind and give students the "okay" to submit a product they want to create. (I always make sure that students understand I may or may not be satisfied with their submissions, and they must agree to refine them if requested.) Be sure to focus students on choosing appropriate means that will help them reach their goals.

Allow students to have input for due dates regarding assignments.

Give students their assignments, and then ask students for some input on the due date. Help them clarify the goals and objectives and think about a reasonable time within which to accomplish them.

Teach students how to manage their own time.

You can help students with this by breaking down large and long-range assignments into smaller, more manageable tasks. Provide short time spans between these smaller tasks so students remain focused on the goal.

ENCOURAGE PERFORMANCE APPRAISAL

If independence of thinking is to lead to new investigations, then students need to learn to evaluate their own performance. There are several ways to encourage this.

Teach students how to write and develop scoring guides or rubrics.

Set out the intended task, and then let students help develop the scoring guide or rubric for that task. When students can become part of the process for performance appraisal, they may be more apt to do better on the task itself.

Allow students to discover solutions on their own.

Independence of thinking leads to new investigations. Provide the time and opportunity for students to figure out solutions to problems and complex situations on their own. Sometimes students will come up with better ideas than the teacher. A simple and frequent example of this occurs when one of my students misses school because of a family vacation. I do not allow students to make up any quizzes, tests, or assignments in this situation. (This is based on my own philosophical beliefs.) I leave the solution to a missed score to the student. I will offer to review the objectives for the missed quiz or assignment. Then, it is up to the student to figure out what to do. (Younger adolescents need more encouragement to think about solutions than do older adolescents.) I require students to provide a potential solution on paper. I review this with the student, and we discuss specific modifications, if necessary, until we both agree on the resolution to the issue.

Give students individual assignments that work toward group goals.

Teach students that by accomplishing individual tasks, a major common goal can be achieved. Give a small group of students individual assignments. Then, show students how they can reach a major common goal if everyone accomplishes his or her own task. For example, within one group of students, I assigned one student to use the computer to research background information on a person the student needed to know about. Another student was given basic information on the accomplishments of that same person and was asked to illustrate, or in some way design a graphic, that represented the person's accomplishments. Another student was assigned the job of outlining the information about this person found in the textbooks that all students had available. Once all three students accomplished their tasks, they were asked to organize their information into an oral presentation to the whole class. As long as each student successfully accomplished his or her individual task, the final job, that of giving an oral presentation as a group, was fairly easy.

Allow students to write or design their own "tests."

I have found over the years that by allowing students to design their own tests, not only have students reinforced their own learning, but they tend to challenge their classmates with test items which have more difficulty than I might have designed.

Teach students to evaluate their own work.

Design checklists for students which they can use to evaluate their own work. Teach students to read and check off each item on the list before submitting their work for teacher evaluation.

Accept student critiques, showing students how to be self-critics.

Let students use a scoring guide, checklist, or similar performance appraisal to critique their own work. Since "letter" grades are still most commonly used for indicating an accomplished level of performance, have students assign themselves a "grade" for their work. Then, require that students provide a rationale for their decision. Accept what students do.

Teach students to reflect and write their own learning diaries.

Give students time to write what they are learning; not just information, but the process of becoming independent learners and self-critics. Provide stems for students in guiding them to respond to appropriate avenues of thought for this process. Examples of stems that might be used could include:

- I learned that . . .
- I didn't know about . . .
- I now know that . . .
- I never knew . . .
- I now understand that . . .
- I wish I knew more about . . .
- I feel . . .
- I think . . .

Have students write self-progress reports.

One of the best learning experiences for students is to write their own progress reports. I have had my own students from middle school to the college level write their own progress reports, and students are much more realistic about what they know and can do than I think teachers give them credit for.

PROVIDE FOR SELF-REINFORCEMENT

The ultimate goal of schooling for students is that they develop the internal motivation to succeed. Students need opportunities for self-reinforcement that will nurture this internal motivation. Some suggestions for teaching and encouraging self-reinforcement follow.

Provide students an opportunity for individual or independent study.

Students will become independent learners if they are provided the opportunities that encourage it. Some students will need more guidance than others. But students should be given the chance to learn on their own, to pursue learning objectives in their own ways, and at their own pace.

Let students develop their own "review" or reinforcement activities.

For the most part, students know what they need in terms of reinforcement. Give students the time and opportunity to develop their own activities like games, puzzles, and other activities that reinforce or review previously learned material. Check Internet resources which students might use, like www.puzzlemaker.com. This site allows a person to insert vocabulary words, and then it creates a workable puzzle with them.

Teach students to pace themselves.

Give students their assignments with enough lead time that you can provide timely reminders that encourage students to complete their work by the due date without procrastinating and then "cramming" at the last minute. Simple verbal cues like "by the end of today's class, you should be at (such and such a point) with your assignment (or project)." Or, better yet, for work that should be accomplished over several days, create a calendar that students can use as a reference. Then simply remind students to look at the calendar and point out on the calendar at which stage students should be in their work at any particular time.

Allow students to choose their own rewards for reaching goals.

Students need to learn that reinforcing themselves for accomplishing goals is a motivating experience. We have all rewarded ourselves with something after reaching a goal. Allow students to make a list, or menu, if you will, of rewards that are meaningful and for which they will work. The behaviorists love this approach. Asking students to tell you what is meaningful to them as a reward is the easiest way to find out for what they will work. Give students a 3″ × 5″ index card on which to write this information, then keep these cards handy for reference.

ROLE-PLAY WITH OPTIONAL ACTIONS

In any given situation, students need to figure out what the consequences are for the choices they make. To encourage students to make independent choices, teachers can provide situations for students to role-play. By providing scenarios where students can choose their own ways to respond, they will learn to make appropriate decisions for their own actions. A few ideas for implementing strategies that encourage more role-playing follow.

Provide the knowledge base for a concept to be learned, then let students make up a scenario for applying that concept.

Bloom's taxonomy (Bloom et al., 1956) implies that students must know and comprehend something before they can apply it. Once students can apply a concept, they are ready to analyze it. This leads to higher-order thinking skills. In addition, students generally learn best by doing something. Therefore, give students time to work together to create role-playing situations that apply knowledge they have gained.

Allow students to form their own opinions and then to express those opinions.

Encourage discussions that force students to form their own opinions. Let students express those opinions as long as students can provide a rationale. All too often, students have no knowledge base from which to form their views. Be sure this knowledge base exists so students can support their thoughts and opinions.

Teach students how to debate.

In addition to supporting their own opinions, students should learn to accept the views of others. Teach students the skills of having an educated debate. This will also reinforce skills of conducting research, critical thinking, and speaking and listening. Students are sometimes under the impression that a debate is an argument. Teach them how to prepare for presenting the issue they support. Teach the importance of researching and anticipating what the opposition might present and being ready to counter. Teach that practice in presenting is advantageous. Show videos of political debates. Ask students to attend speech contests where debates may take place. What is important is to make sure students understand the concept behind and the approaches to successful debating. Avoid the assumption that students know how to debate by teaching and reviewing the skills necessary for success.

Provide time for students to do group work where they can experience having a variety of roles.

There are numerous books available to teachers that serve as guidance for successful cooperative activities with students. A key element for these activities is that each member of the group must serve a specific role that is necessary for the group to accomplish its goal. Teachers can create various ways to assign these roles. The key is to be sure students experience having to fulfill a variety of roles. If a student is a timekeeper for one activity, then that student should be the leader or researcher for another activity.

SUMMARY

Student motivation to learn is increased when students are allowed to think and act for themselves. Independence of thinking leads to new investigations. Learning how to set goals for themselves and reinforce their own independent actions will help students make appropriate choices for themselves. This life skill of setting goals will help students identify what is of value to them and clarify the means of achieving those same goals. Students need to learn to consistently evaluate their own performance. This leads to an honest self-appraisal in attempting to reach the students' own goals. This, in turn, will enhance the internal motivation and self-satisfaction necessary for students to make decisions for themselves in future years.

5 Motivation Is Reflected in Victory

Being successful is moving closer to a goal, not necessarily reaching it.

—Shanley (1990)

S tudents should recognize that progress is directional, not just an end in itself. Educators are responsible for providing an environment that allows students to strive toward success. Growth and development should progress in a positive direction toward the accomplishment of preestablished goals. Donald Eichhorn, a prominent middle school educator, wrote:

> A flexible learning environment enhances stage level mental development . . . experience is an essential ingredient for the growth of mental structures . . . in a flexible environment, youngsters are able to pursue personal curiosity, develop further interests, and increase opportunities for experience by means of a chain reaction effect, i.e. one experience providing the motivation for an additional experience. (Eichhorn, 1966, p. 60)

Helping students recognize and experience situations that make them feel successful should be a major goal for all educators. Two approaches that may assist educators in this endeavor include the following. First, guide students through a process of learning that leads to success. Second, allow students opportunities to create finished products.

PROCESS LEADS TO SUCCESS

An important consideration for selecting strategies that may help increase student motivation is to maintain focus on the processes used in leading students toward success. The process is sometimes more important than the product. When it comes to motivation, process is critical. Consider the following strategies that may assist you in this effort.

Help students form an interest in the topic.

Write a rationale for the topic you are trying to teach, and share that rationale with students. Several points to keep in mind when trying to get students interested in a topic include (a) writing a rationale directed toward the students themselves; (b) including reasons why the topic is important for students in the general scheme of life; (c) stating exactly what students can expect to learn during the unit; (d) being clear about why this topic is important to your students now, in the present moment; and (e) making connections between the skills to be learned during the unit and topics and skills the students have already learned or may be learning in other classes they are taking.

I sometimes hold a class discussion before starting a new unit that addresses these issues. When the students can identify connections between their own lives and what they are studying in school, they are more motivated to learn. It may be helpful to have small groups within the class and have each group brainstorm about a specific segment of the rationale. Then have students share their ideas with the rest of the class.

Find out what students do well, and use that information in class.

If experience with your students has not already helped you identify what your students do well, then a quick interest survey might add information to your own knowledge base about what students do well. With this knowledge, you can connect examples during teaching to the interests and skills of your students. Knowledge of what students do well will also help you identify peer tutors and leaders during specific activities.

Assess student strengths and provide individual enrichment.

Once you know individual student strengths in terms of either knowledge or skills, provide experiences that will add some depth and breadth about the topic for students who are ready for enrichment activities. Sometimes students who already know and can do what teachers set in their objectives lose motivation because of boredom. Challenge these students by offering students a file of various activities. Put this file in a place where students can pick and choose activities for themselves at appropriate times. In my classroom, I used to keep two boxes of activities or directions for activities on the windowsill. One box was labeled "REINFORCE-MENT" and the other "ENRICHMENT." The activities in both boxes always had some relationship to the current unit of study. It was easy to direct a student to choose an activity from one or the other of the boxes. And, because there was self-selection, this procedure had an element of built-in motivation. Generally speaking, students will choose an activity that is challenging, but also an activity they can accomplish with some success.

Give incentives and rewards when appropriate.

Some students will learn and be successful without any additional incentives or rewards. Other students need an occasional boost to maintain some level of motivation. Be cognizant of this need, and be ready to provide additional incentives or rewards to students when you feel it is appropriate to do so. A "smile" sticker, words of encouragement, or some similar positive reinforcement that might be meaningful to the student could help that student stay focused on the task at hand.

Allow students to resubmit their work.

My students learn early in the school year that an "R" on their papers means that something needs to be fixed and "resubmitted" before I'll accept it for credit. Some tasks require mastery. These tasks are appropriate for resubmission. Students learn from their mistakes, and teachers need to allow this to occur. Knowing that errors can be fixed and work resubmitted can increase a student's level of motivation for future work. There is a major trust involved in this procedure. Students need to know that if they resubmit their work and it is acceptable, they will get credit for it. There is a built-in motivator with this process that tells students that if they make mistakes, they will have an opportunity to fix them. And, if they fix their mistakes, they will get credit. Watch what students do with their papers when they get papers back from the teacher with a lot of marks on them. Students typically "file" those papers on the way out of the classroom. Convince students they can resubmit their work if they "fix" their mistakes and you will see a difference in attitude and motivation to continue working.

Let students participate in activities that do not necessarily result in getting a grade.

Students should have experiences that in and of themselves provide some sense of accomplishment. Students need opportunities to engage in activities that help them realize that learning can be exciting! Learning can be motivating! Learning can be fun merely through participation! So, go ahead and give a quiz, have a debate, assess student learning in some way. Then, inform students there is no "grade" attached. Participating is what is important. Try this every so often, and you might find students beginning to enjoy activities just for the experience of the activity. Be patient. This strategy takes time if you want to change the attitudes of students.

Encourage students to participate by rewarding involvement.

Students do not always need to be motivated by a "grade" for their work. But sometimes students need to be encouraged to take an active role. Find ways to reward students for participating, for being involved in class activities. Know your students well enough to give something meaningful to them, whether it is extra computer time, independent work time, library privileges, or just a smile or recognition for participating. Turn this into a game by assigning students to "teams." See which team can have each person on that team participate in some way before any other team accomplishes this process. Watch students as they motivate one another to get involved.

Use "station" learning.

Provide students with opportunities to be successful by breaking down large tasks into smaller activities that students can accomplish at several locations in your teaching and learning area called "stations." Set up numerous stations in your environment and allow students to work from one station to another, accomplishing posted tasks at each station before progressing to the next. Stations need not necessarily be in any special sequence unless you design them as progressions from one station to the next. The only drawback to designing stations that require a specific sequence in building skill development (physical or cognitive) is that each student would have to begin at the first station. Making stations independent from each other eliminates this potential problem. In addition, station learning can be set up for students to progress individually or in teams. Creativity for learning via stations is limited only by a teacher's imagination. The upside to this is that many students can be actively learning at the same time.

Incorporate games.

Students learn and can be successful in game situations. The relaxed atmosphere of playing a game or even its competitive nature can encourage a student to participate, and ultimately, to learn. Who said learning cannot be fun? A teacher does not always need to spend time preparing for a game situation. Let students create games. By preparing a game and its accompanying rules, students will also learn. Be sure to minimize keeping score and maximize attention on participating.

Give students a project, and then allow them to choose their own mode of presentation.

Guide students through the successful accomplishment of a project, but let students decide how they would like to share what they have learned. Posters, PowerPoint, public speaking, writing, and others can be used as choices. The goal is to let students choose the mode of presentation that they do best. The motivation for this is twofold: being able to choose boosts student motivation as does confidence in the mode of presentation itself.

Praise students for what they accomplish outside of class.

A little goes a long way in recognizing what students accomplish outside of our own classes. Effective teachers know that each student is successful at something. A student will try harder in your class if you praise that student for skills the student has accomplished or demonstrated elsewhere, like a role in the school play, marching with the band, or playing on the volleyball or basketball team. The additional motivating factor here is that by acknowledging a student's accomplishments outside of your own class environment, the student knows you care. When students know you care about them, they will work a little harder.

SUCCESS COMES FROM FINISHED PRODUCTS

Helping students maintain a level of motivation that leads them to create finished products is a challenge for teachers. Finishing the project and accomplishing the task are the elements that lead students to feel successful. Some suggestions for teachers follow.

Present a problem or problematic situation to students. Then get input from all students on how to solve it.

Students need to work for resolution of issues to learn and experience success. A specific example of this is the situation in a community near my home where some citizens wanted a stop sign posted. A teacher in the local high school presented the situation and issues surrounding the request to a class of students. Some citizens objected to the stop sign because it would slow down the traffic flow. Other citizens viewed the erection of the stop sign as a safety situation. The students debated the issue and then brainstormed several ways to address the situation. The students tackled this as a research problem and set out to collect relevant data, which led to their recommendations to the city council. The stop sign was eventually erected.

Plan challenging projects and allow students sufficient time to complete them.

Know the skills and talents of the students in your classes and plan projects that will challenge them. The key here is to provide enough time for students to complete these projects. Sometimes teachers will assume students have time outside of class or outside of school to work on a project. This assumption is not always true. Be sure you can give students enough time during class, if need be, to finish projects.

Give students a schedule of when tasks should be completed.

It is a fact of life that students need continual reminding of when tasks should be completed. Teachers need to make sure students have enough time to complete tasks. In the process, remind students frequently to work toward that completion. Keep in mind that students may have difficulty thinking about a project due in two weeks. Students tend to think about right now and tomorrow. Provide students with frequent reminders, and post a schedule on the bulletin board or elsewhere in your classroom for required completion of given tasks.

Help students make their own personal schedules for completion of projects.

Have students write down their own schedules for completing specific projects. Putting the schedule in writing forces the student to make a commitment. Students know better than teachers what they can accomplish outside the classroom, so let them consider the time they can devote to accomplishing given tasks. Students have obligations and activities outside of school, and this may help them recognize available time around their personal schedules to accomplish school tasks. As a teacher, asking to view students' schedules may also enlighten you to other commitments students may have outside your classroom. This process of creating their own calendar will also help students learn and practice the life skill of setting priorities.

Be sure students are forced to use their *minds* in the process of completing tasks.

Sometimes students need to be forced to *think*. As adults, we are often bored with mindless tasks. So, too, if we want students to complete tasks, those tasks should provide some cognitive challenge. Forcing students to think is not always easy, nor is it always stress free. But educators need to push against this resistance in order to force students to develop higher-order thinking skills. Ask: "Why?" "What for?" "How come?" "Explain further," "What do you mean?" and "Clarify." Students may get frustrated with this approach. But if you stick with it, they will get used to the added push and may start elaborating on their responses without extra coaching.

Minimize restrictions.

Unless the goals or objectives for specific tasks require certain conditions for accomplishment, keep restrictions for students to a minimum. Motivation to complete a task can be stifled with too many rules that ultimately hinder success. Keep an open mind. Instead of asking "why?" ask yourself, "why not?" Over the years, I have gotten more flexible in my thinking and have been pleasantly surprised by what my students have produced when I gave them more latitude with which to work.

Relate small assignments to the big picture.
Give assignments that build on one another.

Students need to understand how several small tasks can lead to accomplishment of a larger goal. Teachers need to communicate to students what this relationship is. Knowing that small successes will lead to a larger one will motivate students to continue to work. This is especially important with skill development. In physical education, students are so eager to play the game of volleyball that they do not comprehend the importance of learning basic skills like the bump, set, pass, and spike. It can be boring for students to practice skills unless the teacher creates interesting ways (like using "stations" or "circuit practice") for students to do this. Two things will help students understand the importance of developing specific skills. The first is to let students play the game with little to no instruction. In the most typical of classes, students will experience some frustration. Second, show students a video of the local high school or nearby college team playing competitive volleyball. This should help motivate students to want to practice individual skills as well as practice the required team strategies to be successful.

Students need to realize how important it is to achieving a greater end that they succeed with learning the small skills and tasks along the way. Students are sometimes not patient enough to learn the separate skills of the task before tackling the end product. They want to paint the picture before learning brush strokes. Students want to build the bookcase before learning how to measure, cut, and fit boards. Students want to jump off the diving board before learning to swim. Find ways to show students the importance of learning smaller skills. Convince students that accomplishing the smaller tasks will lead to being successful in the end. In other words, sometimes a task may seem too intimidating for students, and motivation to accomplish the goal is diminished by the enormity of it all. Break it down into smaller, more manageable tasks to keep students from being overwhelmed.

Provide mediated instruction.

When it appears that students need a little help to get beyond a point where they are struggling to finish a task, give a little help, a little direction that will allow students to keep working. Give clues, guidance, and focused direction when needed. Pay attention and know when to intervene and when to leave the student alone.

Constantly reinforce.

Know your students well enough that you can provide the kind of timely reinforcement necessary to help students succeed in accomplishing their tasks. Just as repetition is a form of learning, so also is reinforcement a form of motivating students. Reinforce a student's efforts toward success as often as the student needs it. For some students, that may mean a constant effort on your part.

Offer models that show students what successful projects might look like.

There are times when teachers want to refrain from showing students models of finished work, especially when creativity is part of the criteria. However, when students might be more motivated to complete a project by being able to see what other students were able to do, then sharing as models previous work can be beneficial. Sometimes just being able to see that the project can be done by their peers is motivating enough for students to tackle the project. Be sure that if you share the work of other students with your class, you have obtained permission from those students whose work you are putting on display. (You might also consider getting permission to share a student's work in writing if you intend to use it as an example at a later time.)

Teach students how to create their own portfolios.

Working portfolios created by students can, in and of themselves, motivate students to continue working toward the accomplishment of a goal. By maintaining a working portfolio, students can reflect on previous work they have successfully done and consider the progress they are making toward the final goal. There are numerous books on the market that can guide teachers in helping students with working portfolios. These books can be found at teacher bookstores as well as some of the more popular bookstores located in and around shopping malls. In addition, teachers can find success stories with the implementation of working portfolios in professional journals and on the Web.

SUMMARY

Students are motivated when they feel a sense of accomplishment. However, it is not merely finishing something, but the process that leads to an end project that can provide the motivation to succeed. Guiding students through processes that lead to success by focusing on student interest and effort will help students maintain the internal motivation needed to continue working toward an end. Ultimately, being allowed opportunities to create finished products provides the sense of accomplishment students need to experience success.

6 Motivation Involves Action

I hear and I forget.
I see and I remember.
I do and I understand.

—Chinese proverb

A mong the basic needs of students is that of activity. One has only to observe the amount of time adolescents spend playing video games, participating in competitive and recreational sports, and using Internet activities for personal amusement to know that adolescents are action oriented. Recognizing this, teachers need to modify learning activities that encourage action on the part of students. Harmin (1994) relates five qualities that exist in a classroom that encourage getting the best that students have to give. Students will give their best only when they are motivated to do so. One of those qualities is energy. That is, students are active, busy, engaged, and involved.

I know from talking to numerous teachers over a span of 15 years that the principal's attitude toward active learning makes a difference in whether teachers feel free to create learning experiences for students that require active, physical movement in the classroom. If the principal advocates a quiet, orderly, teacher-focused classroom in order to feel that learning is taking place (and some principals in the 21st century still look for this), teachers in that school will be reluctant to design activities that require students to talk or physically move around the room. I also know that when principals are aware of the goals and objectives for student learning that include some noise, movement, and activity on the part of students, those principals support the efforts of teachers to provide experiences which dictate that students be active and engaged in their own learning.

We know that the more senses are involved in learning, the better students will retain and comprehend. Therefore, if students can hear, see, feel, taste, smell, and involve their hands, they will have a better chance to learn and remember what they learn. Because of this involvement, students should be more motivated to actively engage in their own learning. There are two main things that teachers can do to help students become more active. First, teachers need to provide the opportunities and the appropriate environment for students to be active learners. Second, teachers can set up the situations for more hands-on activities.

OPPORTUNITIES FOR ACTIVE LEARNING

Students like to talk. Students like to work with each other. Students like to be in charge. Students like to move. Given all this, teachers can implement several strategies that require active learning. Some of these can include the following suggestions.

Initiate class discussions.

It is important to remember that an effective classroom discussion can take place only if and when students have some knowledge base from which to draw. There may be situations, however, when you feel the need to engage students in a discussion either before they have had the opportunity to develop a useful knowledge base, or at a spontaneous moment when a discussion might encourage students to think and, ultimately, learn. On these occasions, it is easy to ask, "How do you feel about that?" "What do you think?" "What is your opinion?" Students will usually tell you what they think. This can be the beginning of a profitable discussion.

Have students work together.

It does not really matter if you have formal cooperative learning activities with students performing specific roles which help the group accomplish its goal. What matters is that students be given opportunities to work with other people. So, whether students work with a partner, a small group, or as part of the whole class, actively participating with others is a social learning skill that will benefit students in their daily lives as well as in the world of work.

Require oral presentations.

Speaking and listening are important life skills. If you do not require students to make oral presentations, some students would never do so. You can accomplish this in other ways than by having one student at a time speak in front of the class, which can be very time consuming and, ultimately, boring once you get past the third or fourth speaker. Have students present a report as a group, requiring each member to speak at some point. Or, put students into smaller groups around the room and have one student at a time speak to the small group. So, whether speaking as an individual, or as a member of a group, the idea is to get students to speak, period. I like to put students into small groups, having one student at a time presenting to the group. Students are required to have a handout for each member of the group and are encouraged to use this handout as an outline for their presentation. Students must *talk* to members of the group, not *read* to them. Students have said that presenting to a smaller group is less intimidating than speaking in front of the entire class.

Let students teach.

It has been said, though I admit I do not know the source, that we learn and retain 95% of what we teach to someone else. You know as a teacher how much research and planning go into creating an effective lesson. So, teach your students how to *plan* for a lesson. Then, let them *teach* that lesson. There are several suggestions to share based on my own experiences. Provide a template for a lesson plan for each student. (See Resource E for an example which is based on Madeline Hunter's [2004] model. It does not matter what model you choose, just provide some outline for students to use.) Teach what each segment of the plan represents, from planning the anticipatory set, writing objectives, selecting teaching and learning strategies, determining assessment tools, to the closure activities. Divide the class members into small groups. Allow each group to select a lesson topic (from a list generated by the whole class and approved by you). Then, provide time for the groups to do the researching and planning necessary to get prepared to teach their lessons. Finally, schedule each group's lesson and let students teach that lesson. (Follow up with evaluations of the lesson by yourself, students in the class, and members of the group who presented the lesson.)

Have students conduct interviews.

This activity lends itself to helping students achieve numerous goals. Want students to appreciate someone else's occupation? Want students to gain an understanding of persons who have lived through unique life experiences? Need students to acquire information that can be obtained only by asking people? Interviews can help students achieve these goals. To better appreciate and understand how each person in a school contributes to the overall climate and its efficient operations, I had my students interview the main office secretary, a bus driver, a cook in the cafeteria, and a custodian. (You can alter this list to include occupations represented in the local community.) Help students develop basic questions for the interviews like the following:

- What skill preparation was necessary for your job?
- What is the best part of your job?
- What gets in the way of doing your job efficiently?
- What would you change about your job to make it better?

You might want to allow students to add one or more questions of their own to the basic list. You can invite people to come to your classroom for an interview. Or, you can assign students to seek out the persons and go to them for interviews. Then, ask students to reflect on what they learned, how they felt, and what they thought about the interview.

Give students the chance to role-play.

Get students more actively involved in their own learning by letting them take on the role of a person in the unit being studied or producing a skit to demonstrate a situation. Have students take on the role of their favorite poet, an impressive person in history, or an artist, and develop a monologue introducing this person to the class. Let students reenact a scenario from history, or take on the roles of persons in their own lives in an effort to find solutions or alternatives to problematic situations. The value of role-playing in helping students identify with others and taking an active part in their own learning is immeasurable.

Encourage students to create their own skits.

Give students the opportunity to produce their own skits. Creativity and the opportunity to write, produce, direct, and exhibit a completed skit allow students to be totally active in situations which, ultimately, will help them learn many skills beyond content knowledge. Whether these acts are directly related to a unit of study or a situation in life, learning to organize and be maximally involved will teach students valuable lessons in working with others to actively accomplish a task. This can also provide the self-confidence students need in order to succeed in the 21st century. Both the son and daughter of my best friend have spent their growing-up years play-acting skits with their friends. Over the years, they wrote their plays (and have a wealth of scripts to prove it), designed their sets and costumes, and videotaped the results. The son is now in college. He has a multitude of international friends, has visited and studied in several countries, speaks three languages fluently and is learning a fourth, and is studying international business law. The daughter is in a nursing program at a major university, learning to care for the needs of other people. I am convinced the creativity and freedom to produce works from their imagination allowed these two young people to aspire to bigger and better roles for themselves in life than otherwise might have happened had their parents not encouraged their active role-playing and been patient through the years of cognitive growth demonstrated through their skits.

Plan appropriate field trips.

Unless your school administrators have put a total ban on all field trips, you can still plan cost-efficient trips for your students. There are several issues you need to address to make a field trip meaningful. Be sure to plan ahead. The experience needs to help achieve an objective in the curriculum. You can use a field trip as an experience to introduce a unit of study, as reinforcement during a unit of study, or as a follow-up to conclude or help sum up learning at the end of a unit. In some way(s) students should be required to be actively involved either in the planning, the execution, or the follow-up of any field trip. It has often been said that students will remember *events* more than just reading or hearing information. I still remember a trip to Morton Arboretum when we were studying about plants, trees, and leaves in high school. We learned to identify basic trees before the trip. Then, we walked through the arboretum with our guidebooks feeling pretty good about knowing what to look for and, ultimately, being able to identify the trees and plants we saw. That experience was followed up with a project requiring us to collect and identify various leaves in our own neighborhoods. I still have that leaf collection!

Use more open-ended questioning.

Shift the focus in the learning environment to the students. Teach students to respect the thoughts and opinions of others by asking the students questions that are open ended, questions that have no specific "right" or "wrong" answers. Ask students to explain their responses. Have students support their opinions. Make students think. Get students more involved in their own learning!

Let students create reinforcement, enrichment, and assessment tools.

As a teacher, you are a facilitator of learning. One of the best things you can teach students is to be a part of their own learning. Teach students the basic skills and mechanics involved in creating tests and assessment tools, crossword puzzles for reinforcement or enrichment, diagrams and graphic organizers to clarify information, and charts to help visualize or categorize material. Then let students do these things. One theory of learning states that students learn best when several senses are involved in the process for that learning. Provide opportunities for students to do these activities. (Try using www.puzzlemaker.com for help in designing puzzles.)

Create situations for students to read aloud.

Think about how often you give students a chance to read something out loud in the learning environment. (Forget about the elementary school experience of having each student read a paragraph from the chapter in the text. No one learned or paid much attention to content because you were counting the paragraphs to the one you would be expected to read and were practicing this in your head until it was your turn to read out loud.) Reading aloud is stressful for some students, and you need to recognize this. Create situations that allow students to read aloud in less stressful ways, but still encourage oral reading. Have students read directions for an activity to a small group. Let students who want to read passages from the text, or another reference, do so while those reluctant readers follow along. Consider how often you read material to students. Rather, hand it over to a student to read to the class.

Let students sing or write lyrics for a known melody.

Adolescents use music to help define them. So, capitalize on this and encourage students to sing while they work. Or, let students write information they need to learn from a unit of study into lyrics for a familiar melody, and let them teach this to others. You might develop a better appreciation for the musical interests and talents of present-day adolescents, and the students might develop more respect for you for allowing them to indulge in their own musical interests.

Encourage students to do more active writing.

Find or create opportunities for students to write meaningful pieces. Newspapers, magazines, or professional journals can offer places where students can submit appropriate articles for publication. Letters to editors, politicians, school or city administrators, and representatives can be sent for expressing thoughts and interests on important and relevant issues. Rewriting endings to stories of interest can help students develop the creative skills necessary to write original stories of their own. Consider that you may have a future novelist in your class!

Give students the option to research and then report on that research.

Teach students the skills to be able to research and write reports. During one of my smaller research projects on motivation with young adolescents, a student said that she wished teachers would let students do more reports and research on things and people that students did not know anything about. Teachers could allow a class of students to brainstorm about people, issues, events, and so on that are related to the teaching/learning unit and about which the students have little or no knowledge. Then, students who are interested could pursue investigations on these topics independently, write reports on their findings, and share their information with the rest of the class. Think how much more students would be involved in not just their own learning, but also that of their peers.

Create simulation activities for lifelong skills.

If the educational experience is to help prepare students for life, then teachers need to provide students appropriate simulations that mirror life skills. From activities like balancing a checkbook, calculating interest for a savings account, interviewing for a job, and designing a résumé to learning the skills for starting up a business, participating in mock elections, and writing literary works, the situations are endless. Teachers need only to be cognizant of life skills that might relate to the instructional unit and follow through with providing the simulated experiences for students that will benefit them in the long run. Ask students for new ideas. Sometimes students will come up with suggested activities you never thought about.

SITUATIONS FOR HANDS-ON ACTIVITIES

As the Chinese proverb indicates, if students "do," they will "understand." It is a challenge for teachers to provide situations for students to have hands-on activities. I offer the following suggestions for consideration.

Have students write on the board.

Blackboards, green boards, white boards. Where is it written that classroom boards are for the use of teachers only? Consider all the things that you write on the board in your content area. Now, think about those things that you could have students write on the board for you. Hand over the written objective or agenda for the class to a student and have a student write it on the board. Talk about information related to the topic and let a student write the notes or outline the material on the board. If you use an overhead projector with transparencies, teach students about the care and use of appropriate machines and let students do some of the writing.

Let students create visual aids.

Provide opportunities for students to create visual aids that will enhance and enrich their learning experiences. Most students never outgrow the desire to draw and color, they just mature to creating posters, charts, brochures, pamphlets, and newsletters. (The use of various computer programs these days certainly helps!) Let students compile information from the instructional unit into a visual aid of their choice to share with their classmates. All students will benefit from the reinforcement of information presented visually.

Create experiments or active research investigations.

Teacher bookstores sell basic instructional materials to help teach students the procedures for conducting active research. These materials can be helpful by condensing what can be a complicated process into a manageable experience for students. Consider the situation within your own school or district for providing the stimulus for research. When I was teaching a group of high school students in a university laboratory school, students ventured out across campus to find out how they could eat nutritionally only from what was available in vending machines. Years later, I ran into a graduate student who had been part of that research group. He said he always remembered that activity! I have read numerous articles where students assessed the school's budget situation and then set out to establish recycling programs to save money from what was formerly just waste. Give students a chance to think about and then play a role in active research.

Allow students to pursue the use of alternative media.

Photographs, videos, and documentaries are additional media that may provide students the vehicles for enriching their learning. Students in the 21st century are skilled in using equipment like digital cameras and video cameras. Try incorporating assessments into the teaching/learning unit that encourage students to use these types of media to demonstrate what they have learned.

Use games or let students create games to help them learn.

In an earlier research project with young adolescents, I found that students indicated their desire to play more games to help them learn. Games could be set up to be used individually, with small groups, or with the class as a whole. Students indicated some concerns, though, if teachers considered games for reinforcement or enrichment purposes. Students said sometimes games were too easy or too hard. So it is important to know the skill or ability levels of your students. In addition, students expressed concern about playing games with other students who were poor losers. Teachers need to consider the competitive nature of game play. Some students thrive on a little competition. Other students do not handle competition well. Know your students well enough to downplay the competitive nature of games or encourage it.

It takes time to develop or create beneficial games for learning. As a teacher, you do not have to do all the work. Let students come up with a game idea. Then let them carry out their idea by producing all the materials and rules necessary to play the game successfully. Allow students to teach one another how to play the game. Follow this up with teaching students how to provide constructive criticism. Have the game producer(s) reflect on this criticism. You then have a learning experience for everyone who was involved in producing or actively playing the game.

Provide enough time for practice of skills students are expected to learn.

All too often, we spend time in class introducing new skills to students with little to minimal time for students to practice those skills. Teachers then assign practice time for homework. We cannot assume that students will practice skills correctly outside of class time unless they have been given enough time under our guidance to really learn those skills. From keyboarding and using the computer for various purposes to skills learned in physical education, industrial arts, family and consumer science, biological science, art, and other related subject areas requiring the development of physical skills, we must make sure students have enough time to learn the skills required to be successful. This is especially critical for skills that students need to practice in mathematics, language arts, foreign language, and other academic content areas.

Give students the chance to be creative.

I am sure you have heard people talk about thinking outside the box. Well, instead of having students reproduce an already existing idea to demonstrate what they know and can do, give them the chance to create something new and unique. Think about the depth and breadth of knowledge students would be demonstrating by *planning for* and possibly carrying out the following:

- Designing a floor plan for a house
- Designing a golf course for the high school
- Creating a new recipe and submitting it to a bake-off
- Decorating their own room at home or school
- Landscaping an area for the school
- Making jigsaw puzzles to help other students learn
- Weaving, sculpting, or designing a work of art for the school or city
- Creating an advertising campaign for a local business
- Designing a Web page for themselves or the school
- Building something usable for themselves, their families, or the school
- Planning a wedding or catered affair

- Painting a mural
- Starting or running a school business
- Publishing the works of other students
- Creating a new lab experiment for a science class
- Designing a logo for someone or some team
- Planning and conducting an art fair at school or in the community

Give students the time to think outside the box for other activities that can serve as authentic assessments. These hands-on activities force students to be involved in their own learning while affording students the opportunity to be creative in their own right.

Have students construct fun worksheets that will enrich their own skills and knowledge and also help other students learn.

Students really like the fun and challenge of trying to solve puzzles. Rather than, or in addition to, the available duplicating worksheets that teachers often use, have the students create their own. Let them create mind puzzles, word searches, crossword puzzles, and the like with information that needs to be learned within a given teaching/learning unit. Let students who create the worksheets also try them out with their peers, collect constructive comments, and then readjust or revamp the worksheets into a final product available for future use.

SUMMARY

Active learning strategies and hands-on activities provide students with opportunities for maximum learning and retention. Students will remember events in which they actively participated more than information which they obtained merely by hearing or reading. So, the challenge for teachers is to encourage students to be active learners by providing opportunities for and situations in which students can learn through their own involvement and, especially, through hands-on activities.

7 Motivation Is Increased Through Transfer

Intrinsic motivation is developed through self-regulation of retention and transfer of subject matter.

—Peter and Ireland (1990)

Gagné (1965) says that transfer depends on previous learning. Knowledge is necessary for transfer to occur. One of the goals that educators have for students is that they be able to transfer the knowledge they acquire through their learning experiences to appropriate situations. Gagné (1965) distinguishes two minimum "essentials for transferability," as he calls them (p. 233). The first is that students need to be able to generalize to a wide variety of applications. The second is that students be able to transfer their knowledge to the learning of new knowledge. Hunter (2004) stated that "transfer is one of the most powerful principles of learning" (p. 134). In addition, he indicated that "transfer can dramatically shorten or lengthen the time it takes to acquire new learning" (p. 134).

As students increase their knowledge base, the ability to retain information and retrieve it for use in other circumstances aids in fostering the intrinsic motivation to continue to learn. Gagné (1974) insists that students must be motivated for learning to take place. He says that "provision needs to be made for encouraging the learner to apply his knowledge broadly and in as great a variety of new situations as can be devised" (Gagné, 1965, p. 233).

There are numerous things that teachers can do to help students develop the intrinsic motivation necessary to learn, retain, and then be able to transfer information where and when necessary. Teachers can relate new learning to previous experiences. This can be related to similarities in the environment, the way the learner feels or thinks, or the learning strategies being used (Hunter, 2004). In addition, teachers can adapt tasks to the self-interests and experiences of students. If students find relevance to their own interests in new learning, motivation levels should increase. Teachers can also make abstract concepts more personal, concrete, or familiar to students. Students need to comprehend in order to retain information that they may eventually need to transfer for use at another time.

RELATE NEW TO OLD LEARNING

Finding ways to relate new information to what students have already learned is a key strategy to helping students understand. Students need to comprehend information if they are expected to retain it. Some of the ways that teachers can help students do this follow.

Share anecdotes and stories.

When introducing new material, tell students about situations with which they can identify. If students can link new material to scenarios presented via anecdotes and stories, they will be more apt to learn. Students like stories. (Just be sure you have a lesson plan or outline to follow so you can keep the lesson on track. Students have a way of getting teachers to veer off the subject once the teacher is in a storytelling mode.)

Make connections to other disciplines.

The curriculum in many high schools is planned and implemented in such a way that students view subjects in isolation. It is important that we help make connections across the curriculum for students. Talk to teachers in disciplines other than your own so you know what students will be studying in those classes. When it is relevant to do so, connect what students already know or are simultaneously learning in other classes. Use analogies often. Life is an integrated experience. We need to help students see schooling as integrated learning.

Connect present to past events.

Effective social studies teachers know how to get students motivated and interested in current events by connecting present situations that students can relate to or by which they are impacted with past events that led up to the current situation. If students can make connections between the past and present, perhaps they will develop effective decision-making skills in the future.

Maximize the transfer of personal experiences to new learning.

Survey your students to find out information about where students have lived and visited. Ask students about events in their lives that are memorable. Know what your students have experienced in their lives so you can use those episodes as examples when connecting new information to something with which students can identify. (The advantage to this is that students will also recognize that you know and care about them because you remembered something personal they shared with you.)

Relate your content area skills to life activities in which students are actively involved or interested.

Presumably, you have done some kind of activity and have gotten to know more about your students. Now, take their activities and interests and connect these to new learning in your classroom. If you teach math, connect it to the angles involved in passing or shooting a basketball. Relate science concepts to outdoor recreation and personal health. Connect social studies issues to life in the local community. Think about all the new information from your content area that you can relate to the use of automobiles and trucks, vehicles that are near and dear to the hearts of all adolescents.

Have students discover relationships between present learning and something they have previously experienced.

Make the time or create the opportunity for students to figure out for themselves the relationship between what they are learning and past experiences. Have students think about the topic, concept, principle, theory, or whatever you are presenting. Let them discuss this among themselves in small groups, or write their thoughts individually. Then, have students share their ideas with the whole class.

ADAPT TASKS TO STUDENT INTERESTS

When teachers can adapt the performance tasks of students to the students' own self-interests, they should be more motivated to learn. If students are more motivated to learn, they will more readily retain information that they may need to transfer to situations at a later time. Following are several suggestions for teachers to help accomplish the goal of adapting tasks to the self-interests of students.

Know the likes and dislikes of students.

Find out what students like and dislike. What do they like to read? Not read? What do they like to eat? Not eat? What do they like to do in their free time? Not like to do? Be sure to know reasons for their choices. Make connections with your instructional unit, whenever possible, to the expressed likes and dislikes of your students. It would help if you took an additional interest by reading the magazines your students like to read. Try a food they like but that you avoid. Visit a place your students like to frequent.

Teach in a style that promotes investigation into students' self-interests.

Utilize teaching strategies that promote inquiry, discovery, questioning, investigating, and reflecting. Encourage students to draw conclusions from their own experiences and interests.

Allow students to express in various ways their own views and interests related to new learning.

Have students design a Web page or make a PowerPoint presentation about their personal likes, interests, and experiences as these relate to new learning. Have a class discussion during which students can share ideas. Let students write in personal journals what they think and feel about the new things they are learning.

Be interested in what students have to say.

You have to express interest in students' ideas in order to use their ideas to make connections to new learning. Students need to know that you really care about what they say. Listen. Then, provide oral or written feedback to students so they know you have heard them.

Allow students to help make classroom management decisions.

Include students in decisions that help make the environment in the classroom conducive to learning. Let students help make rules for the class. Ask students for input on due dates for assignments. Have students lead discussions. Allow students to generate ideas for assessments. Let students choose their own topics for assigned tasks. Find ways for students to personalize homework assignments.

CLARIFY THE ABSTRACT

It is difficult, challenging, and sometimes frustrating for students to learn new information when it is too abstract to understand. There are two main obstacles to learning abstract concepts that teachers need to recognize. First, student levels of cognition vary within any one class of students. Some students may comprehend well, yet have difficulty applying the information. Some students might be able to apply new information, yet have trouble analyzing or synthesizing it. Second, teachers sometimes fail to recognize when a concept is abstract, such as when teaching students about metaphors. A metaphor is a simple approach to teaching students about thinking of two ideas in similar ways, yet, nonetheless, it is an abstract concept.

Connect life applications to the instructional unit.

Before students have a chance to ask *why* they have to learn something and *when* they are going to use it, teachers need to be clear about the applications of the instructional unit to life. Students want to know and teachers should be up front about those applications. If we cannot connect what students will be learning during the instructional unit to applications in life, then we need to ask why we are teaching it. Provide a written rationale for the unit to students. If students know how the knowledge and skills they will acquire during the unit will benefit them, they will be more motivated and ready to learn.

Use the media to teach abstract concepts.

Think about how you teach students about honesty, sportsmanship, ethical behavior. It is not easy. Use the media and situations in life to generate discussions about abstract concepts. Newspapers, television news stations, and news-related magazines are super sources. If the issue is sportsmanship, read about coaches', team members', and spectators' behaviors. Situations about honesty and ethics abound in the general news and economic sections of publications. Assign students to do some reading of current events and find situations relating to an abstract concept you want them to discuss.

Provide examples that make a concept more familiar.

Brainstorm with students about examples that provide them with more familiarity with challenging concepts. If you are working with perimeters, have students think about the backyard fence. If you are dealing with area, work with carpeting or floor covering in the student's bedroom. Discussing scale drawings? Use the student's house and furnishings. If you are working with primary, secondary, and complementary colors, use clothing or painting on the walls of a house to illustrate coordination.

Make the concept of time more personal.

Time is a concept that some students tend to struggle with. Work backward to make connections in time—yesterday, last year, the student's younger years, when parents were growing up, when grandparents were, and so on. It is difficult for students to relate to time past. Equally difficult is for students to relate to time in the future. Start from where students are, presently, and help them relate to time in several ways:

- To examples from history as they relate to students' lives, presently
- To due dates for assignments and projects with respect to how much time students have to complete those assignments and projects
- To future application of concepts as they relate to students' lives presently and over time in their future years

SUMMARY

Motivation is increased through the transfer of information. Comprehension is necessary for retention. Retention is necessary for transfer. It is a challenge for teachers to help students retain information in ways that make students want to learn and be motivated to learn so that same information can be transferred in life situations at a later date. Relating new learning to the previous experiences of students is the first step. Teachers can follow up by adapting performance tasks to the self-interest of students. In addition, teachers need to recognize when they are teaching abstract concepts and try to make those concepts more personal, concrete, or familiar for students. Varying cognitive levels of students in any one class make this challenging but not impossible. The ultimate goal is to help students retain information so they can transfer it when needed.

8 Motivation Is Inherent to Individuality

Do not follow where the path may lead; go instead where there is no path and leave a trail.

—Ralph Waldo Emerson

Each individual is unique. Each individual is motivated in his or her own way. Strategies used to motivate one person may not affect someone else. Teachers can create an environment conducive to motivating most students, but if a student is not affected by that environment, the student will not be motivated. Each student needs to know and recognize what it is that stimulates his or her own internal desire to succeed. Students need to know themselves well enough to feel confident and self-assured in what they do. Students are more motivated when they feel good about themselves, and students who feel good about themselves have positive self-esteem and a healthy self-concept. Early on, Coopersmith (1967) said a healthy self-concept leads to success in school.

For some students, getting to a point of self-understanding and self-acceptance is a lengthy process, both in time and effort. Each individual student is important, and teachers need to help each student realize his or her own uniqueness and significance as an individual. Motivation comes from within the individual, and each individual reacts in a different way to stimuli. Therefore, teachers need to be flexible, open-minded, and knowledgeable about students' needs and their growth and development.

Teachers can help students learn about and accept themselves as individuals in several ways. First, teachers can help students recognize their own weaknesses to overcome and strengths on which to build. Second, teachers can directly relate intellectual experiences to the rate and extent of students' cognitive abilities. Bruner (1962) suggests that the ultimate quest for teachers is to develop materials that provide a challenge to the superior student without damaging the confidence and motivation to learn of students who function at the lower levels of cognition. Third, teachers can provide opportunities for students to demonstrate their own individual talents and skills. And last, teachers can encourage the expression of each student's own differences from others. Suggestions follow on how teachers can meet these general objectives.

RECOGNIZE WEAKNESSES AND STRENGTHS

Teachers as well as parents need to acknowledge the fact that each student has weaknesses to overcome and personal strengths on which to build. Sometimes neglecting to recognize their own weaknesses and strengths interferes with students' motivation to chart their own paths to success. Teachers have the opportunities in schools to help students recognize their own weaknesses and find ways to compensate for or overcome them. Likewise, teachers can manipulate the school environment in such ways to help students realize their strengths and utilize these strengths to their advantage. The following strategies may help teachers accomplish this task.

Give students opportunities to self-evaluate.

Make time for students to evaluate themselves prior to teaching a new unit of study. Ask students to address what they already know and can do as well as what they do not know and cannot do as they reflect on the goals and objectives for that unit. Be sure to follow this up at the end of the unit with another reflection based on what the students recognize they have learned and can do. I have taken the opportunity to do this multiple times with both middle school and high school students. Each time, the students are usually surprised by how much they have learned and what they can do at the end of the unit compared to the beginning of the unit. As a teacher you have to find and make the time for students to do this in class. (This is not effective as a homework assignment.)

Let students choose their own roles to play in group activities.

Some students are leaders. Some are followers. Give students the opportunity to choose their own roles in group activities like that of leader, timekeeper, secretary, and so on. (It might be that in middle grades, students need to take on various roles to better recognize their own strengths and appreciate the contributions of others.) But, by high school, students should have some opportunities to make choices about their roles and responsibilities in group activities.

Write comments on student work.

Take time to write comments on student work that recognize what students are doing well and constructive comments that indicate what students need to do to improve. It is extremely time consuming to write any kind of comments on student work, but if we really want to help students improve their weaknesses and build on their strengths, teachers must communicate with students. Sometimes, with an increase in the number of students in any given class, the only opportunity a teacher may have to communicate with a student one on one may be in writing. It is usually easier to comment on student errors and weaknesses. But teachers need to balance this by also indicating what the student is doing well. Students are more motivated to work when told what they *can* do as opposed to what they *cannot* do.

Hold individual conferences with students.

Not all students need to have individual conferences with their teachers, nor is there time to orally confer with each student on any given day. However, some students need the give and take, the oral feedback of a conversation to better understand what their weaknesses are and to figure out ways to improve or overcome them. In these cases, just a few minutes during class (while other students are occupied with their own work) or before or after class or school may be all that a student needs. If you need extended time with a student, be sure to arrange it at a place and time when you will not be interrupted.

Get student reactions to assignments.

Students have suggested to me that I allow time and space for them to write their own comments at the end or on the bottom of an assignment. Though I have not done this as often as I could, when I did, not only have students learned something about themselves, but I have also learned more about them and the structure and expectations of that assignment. Students can indicate all kinds of informative things for you, from what was easy to what proved to be challenging for them, as well as constructive comments for you on how to make the assignment better and more meaningful.

Have students construct portfolios.

There are so many positive outcomes with the use of portfolios. One of the most important is that students learn to recognize their weaknesses and reflect on how they can overcome those weaknesses. Equally important is that students recognize their strengths. In a "working" portfolio, students can measure their own progress. In other kinds of portfolios students can display their best works and show off their strengths as well as what they have learned. The most important part of any portfolio is reflection from students on what they have learned or gained from their experiences.

Give students a chance to brag about themselves.

This can be done orally or in writing. It can be done within the last minute of a class. Just provide a chance for each student to say or write something positive about his or her skills (e.g., I am a good speaker! I am a colorful artist! I am a fluent reader! I am a creative writer! I am a deep thinker! I am an imaginative poet!). Students can write this in a journal, on a memo sheet that you provide, in their own notebooks, or in their school calendars, or they can simply state it in small groups or to the whole class, if there is time. Each person says or writes something positive about him- or herself.

RELATE COGNITIVE EXPERIENCES TO ABILITIES

Students are sometimes frustrated because they are asked to perform tasks beyond their own cognitive abilities. Frustration inhibits motivation. To help alleviate this situation, teachers need to directly relate intellectual experiences to the rate and extent of students' cognitive abilities. Consider implementation of any of the following strategies to achieve this general objective.

Let students choose their own topics for research.

Students really are interested in research. However, one of the comments I have gotten most often from students is that they would like to do research on topics *they* want to know more about. In other words, students want to choose their own topics. I had to do some soul searching on this one to decide whether I wanted students to learn the process of researching or whether the product, based on my giving students the topics, was more important. Since students seemed to be more motivated to research information about topics they were able to choose, that is the avenue I chose. When students have some choice, such as the topic for a writing task, they will be more interested, and consequently, more motivated to finish the task. Their writing will reflect this interest. And in the end, the increase in motivation to conduct research on topics chosen by students spilled over into other activities.

Have students critique works of their choice.

Teach students to be critics and learn the elements and processes for analyzing and evaluating, but let students choose their own works for the process. Students will be more motivated to learn if they have a choice to critique something they have chosen and in which they are interested. If students read comic books, let them critique a comic book; if interested in hot rod magazines, critique an article; if interested in home design, critique a design proposal; if interested in videos, critique a video or a process that was used within the video. Let the students make some choices, and keep an open mind to those choices.

Allow students to choose discussion groups.

Create several small discussion groups, each having a different topic related to the general theme of the unit, and let students choose which topic they would like to discuss. Too often, in an all-class discussion, the same small number of students participates. By creating several small groups for discussion, more students get involved. An additional advantage is that students can choose the topic they would like to discuss and may be more motivated to participate. After a set amount of time in small groups, you can then hold an all-class discussion guaranteed to have more students participating than if you would have skipped the small-group activity. Here is how it has worked for me. (Do "1" and "2" at the end of a *previous* class.)

1. Brainstorm with the whole class for related topics or issues to discuss. Predetermine how many small groups you want, and be sure to finalize the number of topics to this number.

2. Have students individually select two or three topics they would be interested in discussing and write these down on an index card in their priority order. Collect these.

3. With the topics on index cards, create the discussion groups, by topic, making decisions along the way as to how many students you want to allow in each group. (Do this after school or at home.)

4. On the day for discussion, post the small-group members and their respective topics. Give students time to gather in these groups.

5. Give appropriate directions and guidelines for each small discussion group.

Teach the concrete before the abstract.

Students must be secure in learning concrete information before they are ready to tackle comprehension of abstract concepts. For instance, if students are having difficulty with knowing, understanding, reading, and writing metaphors, then you know they are not ready to tackle that subject. Teach about concrete and familiar objects and relationships before advancing to those issues that are not as obviously familiar to students.

Use Bloom's taxonomy in constructing project development for individual students.

Construct more than one format in developing projects for individual students. Use Bloom's taxonomy (Bloom et al., 1956) as a guide for constructing various formats that directly relate to the cognitive development of individual students. Start with a basic project that requires students to acquire some knowledge. Construct a format for students to use this knowledge that demonstrates this accomplishment. Proceed through each of the five remaining levels of Bloom's taxonomy (see Resource B for an outline of the taxonomy), constructing an appropriate format for accomplishment of a project at each level. Assign students the project at their own individual cognitive levels of readiness.

Use a variety of questions for testing.

Remembering that some students are better essay writers than others, and some students do better with objective tests, create test instruments with variety or some choice. You want to provide the best opportunity for students to demonstrate what they know and can do. So, write some objective questions, some essay, some open ended. Even at the university level, students are sometimes given a choice to answer two out of the three or three out of the five questions given. Or, consider the interesting responses to something like "Tell me 15 things you know about the Civil War." (You can always establish parameters such as asking students to include at least two leaders and three battles.) Keep an open mind and vary the items on your test instruments.

Allow students to make up test questions with appropriate responses.

Let students create items that might be used on an assessment instrument and provide all responses that might be acceptable for each item. Teachers know how time consuming it is to develop test items. Let students help with this task, since students must already know something to be able to do this. Requiring students to provide all possible responses also makes students responsible for various modes of thinking, which might produce various acceptable responses. Students are known to be tougher on each other than teachers might be, so you might find that students will stretch the thinking skills of their peers with their assessment items, and that leads to learning.

Have students develop rubrics and scoring guides.

Let students have some input on the scoring and acceptability of their work. Give students the task of determining what might be average, above-average, or superior work. The process of developing their own rubrics or scoring guides will help students recognize the directions and requirements necessary for achieving the level of evaluation they desire for their accomplishments.

DEMONSTRATE TALENTS AND SKILLS

There is probably nothing that motivates students more than being asked to demonstrate their talents and skills. When students figure out their strengths and then utilize those strengths in accomplishing tasks, the recognition for achievement drives up the level of internal motivation. Teachers need to provide the opportunities for students to demonstrate their skills and talents as individuals. Consider the following.

Offer students the opportunity to present their work in ways that showcase their individual skills.

Over the years I have had so many students come up with ways I had not thought of to demonstrate fulfillment of an objective. In one case, I required students to conduct interviews of various people in the school system to better appreciate each person's contribution to the overall effectiveness of the entire educational process. Students were to write out the questions they asked, and these had to be based on required information needed to be obtained from the interviews. Students were to type up responses of those interviewed, and then reflect on what they had learned about the contributions of each person interviewed to the overall effectiveness of the school system. One student asked if he could tape-record the interviews and his final reflections. I had not even thought about that. It was actually a nice change of pace for me to listen to the student actually conducting the interviews.

For another task (actually, it replaced a quiz the student missed), a student asked to write a poem about the material covered by the quiz. Reluctantly (I tried to recall all I believed about alternative assessments), I gave him the okay. His writing was wonderful! He could not have written what he did without fully comprehending the information required. Another student created a game as an alternative to a quiz that could be used by other students for reinforcement purposes.

Did students realize that their efforts were more time consuming than if they had merely done what was asked in the first place? Sure, they did. Were they motivated by a desire to do something different because they had the skills and talent to do so? Sure, they were. Was I, as their teacher, satisfied that students were learning? You bet!

Two other points I need to make are: (1) I became more flexible in allowing students to deviate from required tasks if the student actually expressed enthusiasm for doing the task in a different way; and (2) other students in the class learned that they could accomplish tasks in more ways than one. I only wish I had kept more notes over the years so I could share more of these alternative tasks with other teachers and students.

To encourage students to think beyond the obvious, I suggest you brainstorm with your students about various ways to accomplish a specific task that demonstrates their learning. Try asking students *how* they can do this. Come up with a list of approaches such as the following:

- Make a poster-board presentation
- Design a PowerPoint presentation
- Make a bulletin board
- Develop a written story
- Write a news article
- Produce a video
- Compose a poem
- Direct a short play
- Write lyrics to a song
- Paint a picture
- Sketch a design
- Write a research paper
- Plan a graphic organizer

Then let students sign up for one activity. Allow small groups to work together if several students choose the same activity. You might even limit the options to force students to work in groups. The alternatives are limited only by your students' imaginations. You might even learn about some skills and talents your students have that you never knew about! A bonus to having students submit varying products is that it is much more interesting for teachers to evaluate several different assignments than 30 or more of the same product like a worksheet. This may be more time consuming to evaluate. But if you are more motivated to evaluate what students do because of their unique products, then you will find the extra time much more interesting and well worth it.

Give students the option to choose a role within a group project that would let them use their own skills and talents.

When students have learned how to be successful with cooperative activities, and they have had a chance to be responsible for fulfilling several different roles during these experiences, then give students the opportunity to choose a role in a group that helps accomplish a goal and that allows them to use their skills and talents. For instance, if the project is to write a news article and submit it for publication, then one person can choose to write, one person chooses to edit, and another could do the research. If a project is to publish the poems and short stories of a class, then one person can solicit, advertise, and collect the works from students. Another person can organize the works into a meaningful collection. Another person can do the legwork necessary for getting the collection bound and distributed.

Another way to approach this is to find out the skills and talents of students (a strategy suggested elsewhere) and come up with activities that "fit" the individual skills and talents of students. For instance, I am a great organizer. I have always liked to do scrapbooks, put together booklets of useful information, and similar products. I would be highly motivated to take on this kind of responsibility in a group project.

Post extracurricular activities in your classroom so students can find out about them.

Choose a place in or around your classroom where you know students will look and post extracurricular activities, both school and community oriented. Students cannot get involved in something if they do not know anything about it. Knowing the skills and talents of your students, you can point out specific activities that specific students might be interested in and then encourage their participation. Between the offerings of the school and those within the community, many students can find something that would allow them to develop and showcase their talents and skills. Find information about the local arts council, theater groups, park and recreation activities, and similar community groups and organizations.

EXPRESS ONE'S DIFFERENCES FROM OTHERS

It has been said that a chain is only as strong as its individual links. Our society is only as strong as the individual citizens within our society. Our students are future leaders in our society, and we need them to be strong, self-assured adults. Experiences in school should support the effort to help students be strong, self-assured, and productive adults. Therefore, teachers need to encourage the expression of each student's own differences from others. We need to provide the support for students to know themselves, to think for themselves, and to respect others and their differing opinions in the process. There are numerous strategies teachers can use to encourage the expression of individual differences.

Encourage students to form their own opinions.

Educators want students to think and develop their own opinions and views on issues. Encourage students to express their own opinions, but require that students provide an explanation or rationale for the basis of that opinion. Ask students to explain, to answer the question "Why?" when expressing their views. There is no "right" or "wrong" as long as one has a reason for one's opinions.

Teach students to respect the views of others.

In addition to forming their own opinions, students must also learn to respect the views of others. Explain that differences in opinions and perspectives define character, and if everyone felt the same, there would be little to converse about. Express your own views on issues, but respect the views of students. That is one of the best ways to teach students to respect the views of others, by your own actions, reactions, and words.

Encourage structured controversy.

Given whatever your major content area, from math and science to communication arts or physical education, create situations of controversy related to the unit students are studying. Encourage students to form their own opinions, to take a stand.

One of the simplest strategies to implement here is what I have done and what I have seen other teachers do successfully.

1. Present the controversial situation.

2. Have students physically move to a specific part of the room depending on what view students support relative to the controversy.

3. Conduct a discussion on various viewpoints.

4. Every so often, ask students whose views have changed to move again, to the appropriate part of the room.

5. With students gathered in various sections of the room, depending on what they believe about the controversy, draw closure to the activity by asking students from various groups what they have learned.

Stop and discuss conflicts that arise.

When conflicts arise—and they will—take the time to let students discuss them. Sometimes conflicts arise over differing opinions. Sometimes conflicts arise over misinterpretation. Let students talk it through. If students know they can be heard, they will be more motivated to work through conflict and, hopefully, learn that differences are okay and people can coexist peacefully, even with our differences.

Have students maintain journals.

Give students the opportunity to maintain journals in which they are encouraged to express themselves at various times during the week. Use this as a way for students to communicate with you, the teacher, on a one-on-one basis. There is not enough time during any given school day or week to talk with all individual students about their own feelings, ideas, thoughts, and so on. Journaling is a good activity that allows students to write their views and have someone "hear." In responding to what students write, avoid judgment. Just let the students know you have "heard" what was said. Give advice only if requested to do so.

How can teachers read individual journals of the more than 150 students a teacher may see in one day? Just tell students you will be reading each journal once, sometime during each week. Then, make a schedule for yourself so you can manage this task. For instance, you might read the journals from students in period one on Monday, period two on Tuesday, and so on. Find what works for you. The important thing is for students to express themselves and expect unbiased responses in return.

Provide time for activities that allow students a forum for self-expression.

There are so many activities that teachers can use that would encourage students to express themselves as unique individuals. These might include the following:

- Have students choose an essay, book, or story, or have students choose those that focus on their interests, needs, and abilities.
- Create a day for students to express and share ideas, practices, foods, and similar things related to their own heritage.
- Allow students to organize and create a scrapbook or collage related to something of personal interest.
- Find a way for students to express their dreams for the future.

Gather more ideas from other teachers, activity books, professional development workshops, and conferences. Whenever possible, find a connection from the unit of study with one of these activities so students can make a personal association with a topic being studied.

SUMMARY

Motivation is inherent to individuality. The motivation to succeed, to be the best individual one can be rests with the ability to know oneself. Students need to recognize their own weaknesses and find ways to overcome those weaknesses. Students need to know their strengths and how to use those strengths as a foundation on which to build.

Required tasks for students need to be at levels directly related to the rate and extent of students' cognitive abilities. Students' motivation will increase when they are asked to perform tasks for which they have the ability to succeed.

Students should have opportunities to showcase their talents and skills. Self-assurance and pride in one's abilities can help increase one's level of internal motivation to succeed.

As students recognize their own talents, they also need to figure out for themselves what their thoughts and opinions are and from what sources those thoughts and opinions are derived. Students should be allowed to express their differences from others and, in turn, learn to respect the differences of others.

Schooling is the great leveler in our society, where students come together to learn in a social atmosphere. Yet, educators must help students recognize the individuality in strengths, weaknesses, talents, skills, cognitive abilities, and personal thoughts and opinions that each one brings to the educational process.

9 Motivation Is Rooted in Ownership

Involvement → Ownership
Ownership → Responsibility

If students are involved, they will feel some ownership.
When students have ownership, they will accept responsibility.
If students accept responsibility, they will be motivated.

There are times when teachers feel overwhelmed with all the tasks and responsibilities that go along with educating adolescents. But if teachers would view their roles as facilitators of learning rather than sole providers of information in their classrooms, they would find themselves acting more as partners with students in the teaching/learning process. This partnership requires that students take on more responsibility for their own learning. In order for students to accept more responsibility, they must have more ownership in matters that affect them. If students are to have more ownership, they must be involved.

Weiner (1990) suggests a theory of motivation that considers causes to which students attribute their success. His attribution theory indicates that if students do something well and believe that they have controlled the situation, pride in accomplishing the task results. If success can be attributed to internal factors, motivation is increased. Having some ownership and responsibility for doing well contributes to the intrinsic motivation for students to continue similar behaviors, leading to success in the future.

Among the five qualities that Harmin (1994) suggests exist in a classroom that encourages getting the best work that students have to offer is self-management. Harmin defines this as conditions where students are self-managing and self-motivating, take responsibility for themselves, and make their own choices.

Teachers can help students become more responsible by providing opportunities for students to be more involved in accomplishing meaningful tasks that are necessary for an effective learning environment. In addition, teachers need to involve students in decision making, especially when those decisions directly involve the students.

TEACH RESPONSIBILITY

We cannot assume that all students recognize when they need to exert responsibility, nor can we assume that all students know how to take responsibility and follow through with given tasks. Students need to be taught what responsibility is and how their actions in being responsible affect other people. For some students, the school environment may be the only place they can get involved in, take ownership of, and accept responsibility for their own actions. Teachers can help teach responsibility by getting students involved in meaningful tasks such as those implied in the following suggestions.

Assign roles and responsibilities in the classroom.

Make students responsible for gathering and putting away equipment and materials, whether it be in a classroom, laboratory, library, gymnasium, studio, or wherever students may be learning. Teach students where materials belong and how items used are to be stored. Be firm and consistent with your expectations. In teaching middle school and high school students over the years, my students were always eager to help in this regard. Students need to be responsible for their own learning, and it begins with helping to retrieve materials and equipment they will use as well as cleaning up and putting away the same. There is a trust established when you expect students to assist in this way. That trust leads to the acceptance of responsibility, because students know they have some ownership in helping provide an effective learning environment.

Expect students to help purchase or bring in needed items for projects.

I read an article in the local newspaper that indicated educators spend a large amount of their own salaries for school supplies for their students. In the public schools where I have taught, either budget constraints, purchasing requirements (and the red tape that goes with it), or the unavailability of what I really needed caused me to simply go to a local store and just purchase what I wanted and needed. In the parochial schools where I taught, the money simply wasn't there, so during those years I relied on my already substandard paycheck, my students, and their parents to help.

I found that when students helped provide some of the funds or brought materials from home so we could accomplish a task, the ownership that students felt for the task was exhibited through the care that students took with the materials used and the pride that was obvious in their faces at the completion of the activity.

Teachers need to be careful with this strategy, however. Simply requesting money from students is not the best approach. In this present economic state of some of our country in the early 2000s, some families are struggling just to have necessities for living. The same goes for asking a student to bring items from home. Get to know your students and their parents. Know when you can ask for what. Brainstorm with students about how to obtain materials needed for an activity or project they want. Sometimes, local merchants will donate what is needed if you just ask. Make sure students have some involvement in obtaining extra items they want that the school cannot provide. Involvement leads to ownership. Working to obtain what you need requires responsibility.

Ask students to sign a contract at the beginning of the school year or semester, promising that they will do their best in all work.

If something is put in writing, it implies a commitment. Students will not necessarily learn just because you are teaching. Teach students that they have a responsibility for their own learning by having each student sign a contract attesting to the fact that the student will do his or her best in all work. File these, and use them as evidence, when needed throughout the term, to remind students of their commitment. I always tell my students that I will work as hard as they do. Sometimes they are not working very hard, and I remind them that I am not, either. Responsibility is a two-way street. I need to continually remind my students of this!

Help students recognize each one's best way to store knowledge.

Not all students learn in the same way, which is why teachers are always encouraged to use multiple approaches and strategies in teaching. Students themselves need to recognize that each one learns in a different way than another and that each student has some responsibility for learning. Since acquiring knowledge is the basis for any other learning activity, students need to figure out for themselves how each one can best acquire and store knowledge. Teach students how to create useful memory strategies. Rather than present mnemonic devices and associated pairs to help students remember information, teach students how to create their own tools that can be used in any of their classes to help them attain and retain knowledge. Teach students the process of using key words to help them remember and organize information for essay questions or tests. It is the process involved in developing memory skills, not just the skills themselves, that will help students be more responsible for and successful in their own learning.

Set criteria for projects and grades, and stick to them.

Students need to know exactly what is expected of them. Be clear about the criteria for projects or final grades and stick to those criteria. We fail to teach students responsibility when we alter our expectations after the fact, or we allow students to whine, talk their way to an extension of a deadline, or give in to excuses. Toe the mark. Be firm. Teach students to be responsible for preestablished criteria.

Allow students to teach minilessons.

Let students become more engaged in their own learning. Teach students how to organize themselves and the work necessary to plan for, implement, and evaluate themselves as well as other students in the class for a minilesson related to a topic in the unit plan. Let them do independent research in planning the lesson. Expect students to be responsible for teaching well, telling them you will not be reteaching any part of their lesson. Meet with the students who will be doing the teaching for the mini-lesson to make sure their objectives align with their assessment. Help them focus on using the best strategies for delivering the lesson. Provide your guidance anywhere along the way during planning. Students will not only learn and retain almost all of what they teach during this activity, but they will also learn responsibility for helping others. (See Resource E for a sample template students can use to help them plan a lesson. Alter this outline as you see fit in adjusting the sequence, headings, or activities to align with your own planning approach and the content being addressed.)

When appropriate, put students in leadership roles.

If you truly believe that you and your students are in the educational game of learning together, then you will capitalize on their desire to succeed by putting students in leadership roles. Seize the moment for a spontaneous discussion and call on a student to lead it. When there is a job to be done like changing a bulletin board, choose an interested student to enlist others to help design, make, and put it up. When a student asks, "Why can't we . . . ?" say, "No reason not to . . ." and let that student take charge. When you need help in accomplishing a task, tell students what the task is, how long it will take, and ask for a volunteer or volunteers.

Allow students to work where they are most productive.

This is a strategy that may or may not apply to your students because of school rules or limitations. If it is possible to do so, allow students to do their work in your classroom, the library, computer room, resource room, or even outdoors. Think about where you do your best work, and I bet it is not in a 30′×40′ room with 25 other people. Some students may need to find a more productive environment in which to work. If alternative areas are feasible, give students the responsibility to accomplish their work somewhere other than in the classroom.

Provide opportunities for peer evaluation.

Life presents numerous occasions for us to evaluate one another's performance. Teach students to evaluate performance against a given set of criteria, and then provide opportunities for students to practice this. Making judgments is a difficult task, and the criteria may force students to make judgment calls. If, however, students can provide a rationale for their judgment, their evaluation, then they will be learning a valuable life task.

My students never feel comfortable with this task. I always tell them it is okay to feel that way. Evaluating another's work or performance is *not* comfortable. But if students stick to the criteria in making judgments, they should eventually become more secure about it. Being responsible for judging another's work is never easy, especially for students evaluating the work of their peers.

Whether the work being evaluated is in written form, oral, a construction project, or a physical performance, students need to learn to be responsible for their judgments or their evaluations. So, be sure to require students to provide a rationale, based on given criteria for the evaluation process. For instance, when I ask students to peer-evaluate, I usually provide a simple rating scale (numbers from 1–5) along with a rubric that further defines each number on the scale. I ask students to assign a rating based on the criteria in the rubric. Then, students must provide a rationale, in their own words, for the rating they assigned. This process forces students to make judgments based on given criteria. The process also forces students to think about their own reasons for making those judgments and makes them accountable for their ratings. (Be forewarned: Students will ask if they can assign a 3.5 rating rather than just a 3 or 4. I usually succumb to this if their rationale can support it. However, students may try a smaller fractional equivalent like 3.25, and that is where I draw the line.)

If you want to make this kind of activity more challenging, put students in pairs or small groups. When I do this, I require that all members of the group (or both partners) MUST agree on the final rating that students assign. There must be consensus. This increases involvement, stimulates further discussion between partners or group members, and requires more thinking, since students are forced to share their rationale for ratings with others in the group.

INVOLVE STUDENTS IN DECISIONS

A key element to students getting involved in, taking ownership of, and accepting responsibility for matters that directly affect them is having input in making decisions. Numerous opportunities in schools allow teachers to take advantage of situations where students can become involved in decision making.

Ask students to make rules of order for their own class.

Because each "class" of students is different from any other class, the "rules" for securing the best environment for learning may also be different.

Involve students in making rules for their own class and include appropriate consequences for those who fail to abide by those rules. If students help make their own rules, they will feel some ownership and should accept responsibility for appropriate behavior or helping to secure appropriate behavior of their classmates. Post the class rules and relevant consequences for breaking those rules someplace where students in the class can see them. Keep the rules simple and few in number. Be sure students allow some judgment on the part of the teacher for consequences, or you will wind up with your own version of "Assertive Discipline" (Canter, 1989), which is okay if that is what you want for your students.

As an example of how involving students in making classroom rules might be accomplished, I like to start the school year by sharing with my students what my vision of an effective learning environment is. Then, I put students in groups of three or four (just let students move to their closest neighbors for this activity) and ask each group to come up with their three top choices for rules we should adopt for their class, keeping in mind that "rules" should contribute to maintaining the most effective environment so that everyone can learn. Give students a designated time limit for this activity. When the time limit has been reached, ask one person in each group to stand. (Since students will anticipate that the person who stands will be the spokesperson for the group, I ask the person who is standing to choose another person in the group who will share the "rules" the group chose. This technique adds an unanticipated twist to participation and sets the tone for students to be flexible.) I then ask for a student volunteer (there is always one in the class who will do this) to write group rules on the board. I help guide the volunteer to eliminate duplications as each group shares their rules. When finished, pare these down to a reasonable number, like three to five, by having students vote for rules the class members are willing to adopt. Once rules are finalized, follow similar procedures for deciding on the consequences should rules be broken. (Rules are only as good as they are enforceable.) Ask for a volunteer to create a display for rules and consequences (student choice for a poster, computer-generated visual, or other means). Then, post this display where members of the class can see it at all times. You might want to read *The Essential 55* by Ron Clark (2003) before you talk to your students about class rules. This book will add further insight into what makes an effective learning environment from the experiences of someone who was a national "Teacher of the Year."

Maintain a suggestion box for each class.

Being open to suggestions from students and involving them in decision making can begin with a simple suggestion box for the class. First of all, ask students if they want one available for their use. (If they do not want it, they will not use it.) Then, solicit volunteers to make the box so it is unique to that class. Keep it in the same place in the room all the time. Tell students how often you will read the suggestions and that you will respond to each legitimate one. What makes a suggestion "legitimate" is that it not only suggests doing something, or changing an existing condition, but also includes an idea for *how* it can be done or *what* can be done in lieu of what exists, and *why* the suggestion is being made. To ensure that students provide all the information necessary for a "legitimate" suggestion, create a half-page template and make copies available for students to use (see Figure 9.1). Students might be a little insecure about making suggestions until they get to know and trust you. If students are sincere about their suggestions, they will not mind attaching their signatures. Besides, this also teaches individual responsibility.

Ask students for their input on seating arrangements.

There are two ways of thinking regarding seating arrangements. Each one can include student suggestions. First, consider the arrangement of the desks or tables in your room, or the arrangement of student work stations. (It might be that you have no flexibility with regard to room arrangement. If so, ignore this first suggestion and move on to the second one.) Get input from students on how they might prefer to arrange their desks or tables. Be sure to ask students for *reasons* for their suggestions. Focus on advantages to learning. Second, ask students on an individual basis (a memo sheet or index card will suffice) *where* in the room they would prefer to sit and *why*. Sometimes because of a physical disability a student really needs to sit in the front (a vision problem) or to one side of the room or the other (a hearing difficulty). (Students may or may not tell you about these disabilities unless you make a point of asking or unless knowledge of students' physical impairments is available to you through an office file, the counselor, or the school nurse.)

Also, consider that students learn better in some environments than others. For instance, if I am in a math class, I want to sit in front so I can focus on the teacher and not be distracted by others. If I am in an English class, I do not want anyone sitting behind me because I have trouble thinking and writing with movement behind me. In a class where discussion is a major activity, I would prefer to sit on one side of the room or in the middle so I can feel immersed in the conversations. Not until I got into college did I figure out my learning needs with regard to the location of my desk in the classroom. Consider finding out where your students prefer sitting in your classes. Let them have some input in this regard. You may be

Figure 9.1   Template for Student Contributions to a Suggestion Box

My suggestion is:

This can be done (how?) by:

Why I am making this suggestion:

_____

Student Signature/Date

Response from: _____

(Teacher)

_____

Teacher Signature/Date

enlightened to find that most students will not necessarily choose to sit near their friends, but will choose an area of the room in their "personal comfort zones" for learning.

Involve students in designing a class calendar.

Teachers usually have a calendar or block plan designed prior to the start of class or a new unit. Rather than mapping all this out on your own, involve students in designing a class schedule which includes all major projects and due dates. Students will be more secure knowing what is coming up in the class. If they have had some input on due dates, they will feel some ownership in the class and, hopefully, be more responsible for accomplishing tasks by the dates they helped determine. Laminate a poster board with a blank template of a calendar and use transparency markers to fill in all the information needed. Better yet, while discussing relevant issues with the class, have a student fill in the calendar. Each of your classes can have its own calendar. Post the class calendar where students can refer to it often.

Consider having students make a commitment to work for a specific "grade."

Once you have shared the scoring guide for final grades for a specific unit, consider having students commit to work for a specific grade. Putting goals in writing helps students be more responsible for achieving them. If students commit to working for a grade you feel is too low, you can do some individual counseling and maybe intercept a personal problem before it really materializes. You might allow students to alter their commitment as time moves along with mutual (yours and the student's) consent. Students need to be involved in decisions that affect them, and their "grades" certainly do affect them. I have asked students at various times throughout a grading period to reflect on their learning. For instance, ask students at the beginning of a grading period to write down the "grade" they hope to earn by the time report cards are due. (For some students this is a "timing" issue, and report cards that are not due for six to nine more weeks are an eternity away.) Be sure to have students tell you *why* they wrote down that grade. You can have students repeat this process of writing a "goal grade" and reflecting on it as often during the grading period as you think it might be profitable for the students. Always have students formally affix their signatures. This adds an extra element of ownership and self-responsibility for earning grades. (Some students have the mistaken notion that teachers give grades instead of accepting the fact that students earn their grades.)

Save all "goal grades," because it might be worth having students review what they had written at the previous time and reflect on whether they are progressing toward their goals or what they need to do if regression is apparent. For some students this activity might be helpful on a weekly basis. For other students, it might be necessary only at the beginning and end of each separate unit of instruction.

It has become a habit of mine at the end of a grading period to ask students to look at the rubric for final grades, determine what their grades are, and reflect on whether this grade is what they deserve. I then ask students to explain why they earned that grade, or, if they earned an otherwise different grade, to explain further.

Students are fairly honest when given the chance to have some input on grades. Having to write down a grade they may have earned and explain why, or explain why they feel they deserve a different grade, extends responsibility for their own learning.

This process may seem too time consuming, but it is not. You should also try your own approach to having students sign a contract or otherwise commit to working for a specific grade and see if, indeed, students take ownership for what they do and, consequently, responsibility for their own learning.

Solicit student input for projects and activities that will help students achieve the goals and objectives for a specific unit.

Present goals and objectives to students for a specific unit of study. Then, solicit their input for projects and activities that will help them achieve the goals and objectives for that unit. Brainstorm ideas with them. Give students additional time outside of class to think about this before making any final decisions. Maintain guidelines, but be flexible in allowing students to make or suggest variations in ideas for projects and activities.

Put decisions to a class vote.

There is nothing better in teaching students how important the privilege and opportunity to vote can be than voting in class on an issue relevant to students. Whenever the opportunity arises, seize the moment to present the issue at hand to a class vote. You can have students decide ahead of time, based on the issue, how much is needed for passage (a simple majority, two-thirds majority, etc.). There are several approaches to voting that can be used: the raising of hands, secret ballot, deciding within small groups and submitting a "group" vote, and so on. Make this act of voting dramatic (or not) as you wish. (As long as the reality show *Survivor* is being televised, capitalize on the drama involved in writing out a vote and inserting it in a special container.)

SUMMARY

Motivation is rooted in ownership. Students are more motivated when they can be involved in accomplishing meaningful tasks that directly affect them. If students are involved, they will take ownership for what they accomplish. Teachers need to take advantage of and create situations that allow students to take ownership of what affects them in the learning environment. Hopefully, this will lead students to also accepting responsibility for that environment.

10 Motivation Is Natural

Challenge your students to learn something everyday that they aren't required to know.

—Shanley (1990)

S tudents have a natural curiosity and will try anything. Motivation is natural, built-in, and innate, if you will. Curiosity, emotions, and basic instincts for survival are just a few internal factors which motivate our actions (Deckers, 2005).

Generally, we think of motivation as being extrinsic (when what we do is driven by external factors like praise and reward) or intrinsic (when what drives our actions comes as a natural desire from within ourselves). Intrinsic motivation is a desired goal in education for our students.

Students are intrinsically motivated when they are interested in a subject or find usefulness and value in what they are learning. Glasser (1990) says that students must view their work as beneficial to them if we expect them to do quality work. He says that the more important students think something is, the more they will do what they are asked, and the better they will do it.

Students in the early elementary grades naturally exhibit motivation through their energetic and enthusiastic actions and attitudes. Along the way to the middle and high school years, some students lose that natural enthusiasm for learning. Other students maintain acceptable levels of motivation either because of, or in spite of, teachers and the school environment. Yet, other students need a continuing undercurrent of reinforcement to maintain the motivation needed to learn all they can while still in school. There are several strategies teachers can use to encourage the natural desire to learn that comes from within each student.

Teachers can help provide an environment conducive to increasing the natural desire for students to learn by challenging students. Success-oriented students are motivated by challenges and the anticipated emotional rewards received from engaging in new tasks (Marzano, 2003). Create situations that force students to think and discover solutions for themselves. Provide time for students to express their thoughts. Encourage students to think independently and work out for themselves the rationale for their own opinions. Acknowledge what students have to say in ways that support their desire to formulate their own views and also respect the opinions of others.

CHALLENGE STUDENTS

When students are challenged to think and perform, they will be more motivated to learn. Teachers need to provide learning activities that excite students and help increase their natural curiosity and desire to learn. Some suggested activities follow.

Vary the use of different teaching techniques.

I could probably have listed this suggestion in each chapter of this book. And perhaps there is an implication from the suggestion to vary your teaching strategies in each chapter, anyway. That should tell you something. If what we want to do is not merely teach, but really help students learn, then we must use multiple strategies in an attempt to address the various learning styles and cognitive levels of the students in our classes. For instance, use informal lectures with media or visual aids to transfer information and set up other learning activities. Moving students into a discussion can prepare the groundwork for a problem-solving situation requiring inquiry. Combining skill practice with games and simulations will help meet the needs of different types of learners. Skillful questioning used with other strategies will promote logical thinking and reasoning abilities. Challenge students to find ways to make learning fun and exciting. Ask students to come up with strategies that might challenge them and help them learn. Remember that teaching and learning should be complementary.

Put problems or situations on the board for students to solve independently.

Challenge students to figure out a problem or find a solution to a situation that may or may not have anything to do with what they are required to know for the unit of study. Sometimes your textbooks can be used for sources of these items. Search the Internet for ideas. Look for materials available in bookstores that are loaded with items you can use with students to stretch their thinking skills. Or, simply put one or two new vocabulary words on the board that students may be unfamiliar with and challenge students to learn about them. Or, write a fact on the board which you think they may not know and enlighten students about something new.

Give assignments that require students to think critically.

Before students can feel secure about situations that force them to think critically, they need to know how to do it. There is a process involved in learning how to think critically, and all too often teachers assume that students already know it. I have made suggestions elsewhere in this book as to how this can be accomplished. Be sure to follow up this learning process with assignments that require students to use critical thinking. Teachers will find useful suggestions for assignments in the students' textbooks or in the teachers' editions for those texts. Pay attention to these helpful items and take the time to use suggested critical-thinking approaches with your students.

Use case studies to help relate the content to situations in life itself.

Set up case studies or present scenarios in life that will help students make connections from what they are learning to their own lives. A more challenging approach would be to have the students write, research, or find case studies or situations that apply to what they are studying, and let the students present these cases to their peers for continued discussion.

Put students in groups of varying interests and abilities.

This suggestion is not merely to put students in working groups, but to deliberately form groups of students with different interests and abilities and present a challenge to solve, a goal to reach that forces a consensus among them. Life situations force people with differing interests and abilities to work together to do strategic planning, make decisions about financial spending and acquisitions, and make various decisions that affect the successful operations of groups and entities in the community. Students should learn the skills involved in working with others of varying interests and abilities and making decisions for the common good.

Let students discover for themselves how problems can be solved.

It is so easy for teachers to help students figure out solutions to problems or situations. It is not so easy to sit back and let students figure things out for themselves. Case in point: Over the course of the last few years, as the use of the Internet has become more and more prominent, I had to learn computer skills that, ultimately, allowed me to be more efficient in my work. A couple of my colleagues were very helpful. However, when I solicited their assistance with my computer, they tended to take my mouse away from me and proceed to click their way around to what I needed to do. They weren't patient enough to let me click my own mouse. I did not learn until I did it myself. In another situation, during a professional development workshop on the use of computers in developing Web pages, the leaders clicked around so fast that I and several others in the group could not keep up. I asked for the leaders to slow down, but they indicated that they would not have time to get through the entire process if they went any slower.

Now, put these situations in your classroom. Do you let students discover and learn on their own? Do you provide enough time for learning to take place? Are you so concerned about getting through the curriculum that you cheat students out of the time and attention they need to really learn? Slow down. Be patient. Let students discover and learn for themselves.

Provide enrichment activities for students who need them.

Nothing stifles the natural motivation of students more than when they are forced to stay in one room with 25 other adolescents and nothing to do. Always have enrichment activities readily available for those who need them. This has been stated earlier in the book, but it bears repeating here. Students who know, understand, and can apply the concepts addressed in a given unit of study need to be challenged further. Keep a file, a box, some tangible container filled with activities or the directions for activities that students can choose from when they find themselves with extra time. Let students choose these activities for themselves, because students will know best what can be motivating or challenging for them.

Have students help set their own goals and be actively involved in striving to reach them.

The school district has goals set for students. Teachers have goals for their students. The students should have goals for themselves. Have students help set individual goals for themselves, either at the beginning of the school year, the beginning of a new semester, or the beginning of a new teaching/learning unit. Teach and encourage students to set goals beyond what they think they can reach. Emphasize to students that making progress toward achieving goals is what is important, not necessarily being able to reach them. Be sure students write these down in a place where they can occasionally review them to check on their progress toward their goals. You can formalize this strategy by having students sign their sheet of goals and date it. Then, you, as the teacher, sign it also. Establish an approach where students can alter or eliminate a goal only with mutual consent of those who signed it. This creates a situation for discussion between teacher and student. The student will also take the exercise of goal setting more seriously and responsibly.

Challenge students to create original projects using technology.

The most compelling resource I found that would inspire students to create original projects using technology is an article titled "Top 10 Innovative Projects" by McLester et al. (2003). This article describes 10 original projects that required collaboration, critical thinking, and in-depth investigations and that had global implications. Among these projects were the following:

1. A wartime documentary: Japanese Americans

2. Virtual marine biology (marine research)

3. Life in the streets (an inside look at issues of homelessness)

The authors indicated that a high student motivation factor existed with these projects.

Provide opportunities for students to earn extra credit.

I have to admit up front that I do not, philosophically, believe in the concept of extra credit. I include this strategy at the insistence of my students. Personally, I believe that if students take the time and effort to do what is expected, there is no need for *extra* credit. For some reason, my students in our teacher preparation program think that some adolescents are motivated by doing something that appears to be "extra," above and beyond what is required. So, okay, I concede that if you want to label something "extra credit" because it motivates your students, then that is your decision. I do not necessarily oppose the concept. I just do not practice it myself.

ENCOURAGE STUDENT EXPRESSION

Students will have a better sense of themselves and be more motivated to actively participate in class activities when they know they can express their thoughts and opinions. Teachers can support this by providing time for students to express their thoughts, either orally or in writing. Consider the following strategies.

Allow time for journal writing.

I realize this suggestion has been mentioned previously in this book. But consider that there are many different types of journals, including gratitude journals, experience journals, daily journals, wishful journals, and more types that you might pick up from your students and in reading professional journals. Take some time to discuss the reflective element that is so basic to any type of journal. Let students decide for themselves what type of journal is best for each of them as individuals. Then, allow time for students to write in their journals. Remember that journal writing is not confined to English or Communication Arts classes. The fine arts, mathematics, science, physical education, foreign language, and other curricular content areas also lend themselves to journal writing, since the idea is to encourage students to express their thoughts. During my earliest years in the teaching profession I served on a "writing across the curriculum" committee for the school district. I practiced what I preached. I managed to find multiple ways to have my students write during their classes of physical education and learned so much about my students and their learning through their writings. I know from student writings that they also learned more about themselves.

Solicit student opinions.

Encourage students to express themselves by soliciting their opinions whenever possible. Most middle and high school students will always have a response to a question like: "What do you think?" or "What is your opinion on that?" Even if students lack a knowledge base to actively and effectively participate in a discussion, they will at least have thoughts and opinions on a topic or issue. Integrate their thoughts into class discussions. Students are more motivated when they know that what they say will be heard without being judged or criticized.

Form panel discussions.

Have small groups of students choose a topic related to the unit of study and form a panel discussion where students voice their opinions and ask questions of one another with minimal feedback or interference from the teacher. Panel discussions allow students a forum from which they can express their thoughts on a topic or issue to one another. Solicit students' input for the rules and guidelines for the panel discussion. I would suggest that students sign up for topics so everyone has a chance to participate as well as being motivated by the process of choosing a topic relevant to the unit which is also of interest to them.

Provide opportunities for anonymous comments and appropriate feedback when called for.

So often, teachers ask students during a class for comments and feedback in a general way and get little to nothing in return. Some students do not want to express what is on their minds in front of others, and sometimes students would rather not be identified with their comments, however mature and legitimate those comments might be. So, provide opportunities for anonymous comments and appropriate feedback when called for. You may want to know what students thought about the day's lesson. You may want to know what students think about an activity or strategy you are thinking of implementing. You may want to know what students think about a topic or issue you may or may not include in a class discussion.

Provide memo sheets, index cards, or similar small papers on which students can tell you what they think. After reading student opinions, provide feedback. Students need to know they have been heard, and students need to have closure. So, be sure to follow up on their comments in some way. Write back on their note cards or talk to students privately. Students will be more motivated to express themselves again the next time you inquire if they know you paid attention to what they previously wrote and took the time to respond.

For example, sometimes I try a new instructional strategy and warn students ahead of time. (Students are more forgiving if I do this and the strategy fails to accomplish what I had hoped for.) At the end of class, I give students 3" × 5" index cards and ask them to tell me their opinions regarding the strategy. If the strategy included group activities, I might ask for feedback from the group as a whole. I read what students write and tell them at the next class that I appreciate what they had to say. I refer to some specific comments so students know I really did read what they said and let students know that I found a way to amend, revise, or actually repeat the strategy again. Then, when I really do try the same strategy in the future, I start off by reminding students of their previous constructive comments and show or tell them what changes I made based on those comments.

ACKNOWLEDGE STUDENT VIEWS

If teachers want students to think for themselves and to express those thoughts, then teachers need to be ready to acknowledge the views of students without judgment. Students do not always need teachers to comment on what students have to say, they only need teachers to acknowledge their points of view. There are several things teachers can do to acknowledge what students have to say and do in ways that motivate students to think, form their own opinions, and share those opinions with others.

Use current events to encourage students to think and express those thoughts.

Every curricular content area has issues that lend themselves to some controversy. In physical education there are issues of health-related fitness and childhood obesity. In mathematics or economics, the buying and selling of stock; the current tax situations at local, state, and national levels; and the buying and selling of consumer goods are controversial. In the fine arts, national funding is a hot topic. You can identify issues related to other areas. So, use these topics and share ideas with students that go "against the flow." Be a devil's advocate. Bring in, or have students bring to class, magazine and newspaper articles that lean to one point of view or another. Use student experiences to present viewpoints. In any case, encourage students to think and express their thoughts without necessarily commenting or focusing on one point of view more than another. Definitive closure is not necessary. Just push students to think. Accept all valid contributions provided, as long as students include the rationale or reasoning behind their input.

Make time to have a class discussion on subjects that are personal and important to students.

Allow enough time for students to express their thoughts, opinions, and feelings on topics that are personal and important to students. It does not matter what curriculum content area you teach, there are numerous opportunities throughout the school year when, if you seize the moment, students need to take some time out to talk. If you are concerned about educating the whole child, the adolescent in all of his or her growth areas, then you will make time to let students find out that their peers are sometimes experiencing similar thoughts and feelings. It is natural for adolescents to think they are alone in what they think, feel, and are experiencing. Let them find out that others feel and think the same, and that others are experiencing similar situations. Students will think. Students will listen. Students will talk when they know you care. One way to let students know you care is if you will find out what is personal and important to students. When students know you care enough about their personal issues, they will be motivated to do almost anything else you ask of them.

Allow enough time at the end of each lesson for discussion of the day's lesson or topic.

Ask students for some input on their thoughts and opinions of the day's lesson or the topic that was the subject of the lesson. Effective teachers always reflect on the daily lesson in an effort to either improve aspects of that lesson or find better ways to direct lessons that follow. Capitalize on the natural desire of adolescents to express their opinions on what affects them and their learning by asking for some feedback from them about that lesson. Let students share in the reflection of a lesson. Remember, we are all in this game of education together. Including students' views in your closure of a lesson will give you an opportunity to acknowledge what students have to say without necessarily commenting in return. Remember to ask students about the materials used for the lesson, too! Just take it all in. You do not need to defend yourself or comment. Just be open to what students have to say.

Ask students open-ended questions.

Whether orally or in writing; whether on a quiz, test, or alternative assessment; whether during a class discussion or personal inquiry, find ways to ask students open-ended questions. The nature of open-endedness allows students an avenue to express what they have to say in their own ways. It is more motivating for students to respond when they know they can do it in their own way(s). Just think about how frustrating it is to complete a written survey with forced choices that do not allow you to express what you would really like to say. Then reflect on how much more motivating it is to respond when there is space for additional comments, or open-ended statements, that allow you to share your honest and real thoughts and opinions. Provide opportunities for students to respond to open-ended questions.

Be natural.

Just as you want to capitalize on the motivation that comes naturally to many students, so also should you be natural in expressing acknowledgment for what students have to say without necessarily offering a commentary in return. Smile. Use appropriate, positive body language. Be yourself.

During a backstage tour of Disney World, I learned that cast members are taught to use an open-handed, palms-up gesture to show people the direction toward what they want to see or where to go instead of pointing with a finger. Also, two hands with both palms up were used to encourage people to participate. I made a concerted effort in my classes to adopt these gestures in acknowledging a specific student (one hand) or in acknowledging contributions from students and requesting more participation (two hands). After a period of time I asked students to comment on my use of these gestures, and they indicated that the gestures expressed a more "welcoming" and friendly attitude on my part. Try it. Make these gestures a natural approach on your part in requesting more student participation. The important message here is to be natural. Be yourself. But be open and welcoming to the natural desires of students in wanting to learn.

SUMMARY

Motivation is natural. It comes from within a person. Levels of motivation can fluctuate in any given situation. Students have a natural, innate desire to learn. That desire to learn must be nurtured. In so doing, teachers need to provide situations in which students are challenged—challenged to think, to discover, to perform. Students need to know that what they think is important, that their opinions matter. They need a forum for expressing their thoughts and views. They need an atmosphere in which students can make choices and discover for themselves the joy of learning.

Resource A: Strategies and Learning Styles

VISUAL LEARNERS

Characteristics:

Like to: see, write, make lists, draw, color, doodle, read, talk, visualize, organize

Strategies:

Use: graphic organizers, exhibits, computers, posters, visual media, bulletin boards, demonstrations, charts, graphs, diagrams, manipulatives, flow charts, concrete examples; model intended behaviors, problem solving, cooperative activities

AUDITORY LEARNERS

Characteristics:

Like to: hear, listen, read (especially to him- or herself), need quiet atmospheres for study, enjoy music for pleasure, but not during study, listening to others

Strategies:

Use: lectures, repetition, discussions, audiotapes, reading aloud, verbal instructions and directions, skill practice (alone)

KINESTHETIC LEARNERS

Characteristics:

Like to: touch, feel, be physically involved, be active, gesture, move, construct, produce, manipulate, use any hands-on activities

Strategies:

Use: role-playing, station work, media, experiments, projects, simulations, problem solving, manipulatives, dimensional products, games, cooperative activities

Resource B:
Bloom's Taxonomy,
Cognitive

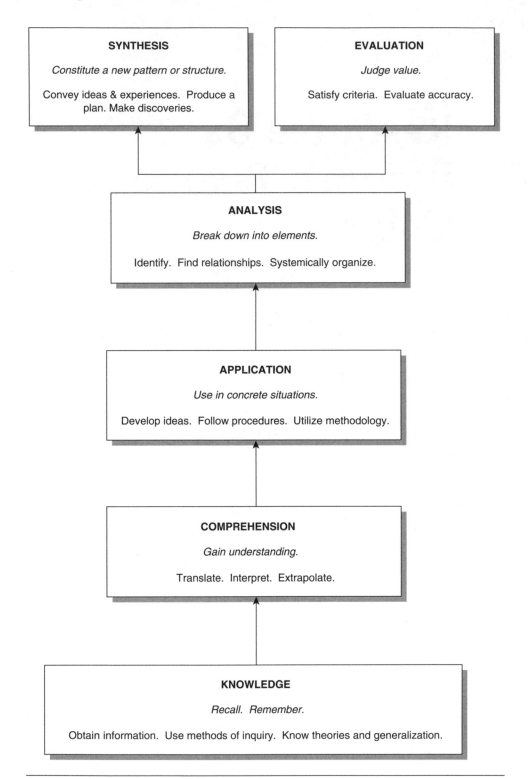

SOURCE: Adapted from Bloom, Englehart, Furst, Hill, and Krathwohl (1956).

Resource C: Positive Word List

A
Able
Accepting
Accessible
Accommodating
Active
Adventuresome
Affable
Agreeable
Alert
Ambitious
Amusing
Analytical
Appreciative
Approachable
Artistic
Assertive
Astute
Attractive
Aware
Awesome

B
Beautiful
Big-hearted
Bold
Brainy
Brave

Brief
Bright
Bubbly
Bustling
Busy

C
Calm
Capable
Careful
Caring
Cautious
Certain
Charitable
Charming
Cheerful
Clear
Clever
Comical
Compassionate
Competent
Composed
Concerned
Concise
Confident
Congenial
Conscientious
Considerate

Content
Cool
Cooperative
Creative
Curious

D
Daring
Decision maker
Deductive
Delighted
Delightful
Democratic
Dependable
Determined
Devoted
Different
Direct
Discreet
Distinctive

E
Eager
Easy-going
Effervescent
Efficient
Elated
Empathic

Encouraging
Energetic
Enthusiastic
Exciting
Expressive

F
Fair
Fascinating
Fast
Feeling
Firm
Forgiving
Friendly
Fun-loving
Funny

G
Generous
Gentle
Gifted
Giving
Glad
Glowing
Good
Good-looking
Good-natured
Graceful

Gracious
Grateful
Great
Growing

H
Handsome
Happy
Healthy
Helpful
Honest
Hopeful
Humane
Humorous

I
Imaginative
Important
Impulsive
Independent
Inductive
Industrious
Innovative
Inquisitive
Insightful
Instructive
Interested

J
Jolly
Judicious
Just

K
Keen
Kind
Knowledgeable

L
Leader
Liberal
Likable
Liked

Lively
Loved
Loving
Loyal
Lucid

M
Mathematical
Merry
Mild-mannered
Motivating
Musical

N
Natural
Neat
Nice
Nimble
Novel

O
Objective
Obliging
Open
Open-minded
Optimistic
Orderly
Organized
Organizer
Original
Outgoing

P
Patient
Peaceful
Perceptive
Perky
Persistent
Persuasive
Pleasant
Poetic
Poised
Polite

Popular
Positive
Practical
Pretty
Productive
Proficient
Progressive
Proud
Prudent
Punctual

Q
Qualified
Quick
Quiet

R
Radical
Rational
Realistic
Reasonable
Receptive
Refreshing
Reinforcing
Relaxed
Reliable
Reserved
Responsible

S
Satisfied
Sensible
Sensitive
Serious
Sharing
Silly
Skillful
Smart
Sociable
Speedy
Spontaneous
Stable
Strong

Succinct
Sure
Swift

T
Tactful
Talented
Talkative
Tenacious
Terrific
Theatrical
Thorough
Thoughtful
Tolerant
Tough
Trusting
Trustworthy
Truthful

U
Understanding
Unique
Untiring

V
Vigilant
Vigorous
Virtuous

W
Warm
Watchful
Wholesome
Willing
Wise
Wonderful
Worthy

Z
Zeal
Zealous
Zest

Resource D: Example, Student Goals

Name: _____

Unit Title:

_____

Knowledge and skills to be learned:

Choose as many of the above items of knowledge and skills, and for each one, write a goal for yourself that you will strive to reach by the end of the instructional unit.

Knowledge or Skill	Goal for yourself
1.	
2.	
3.	
4.	
5.	
6.	

Resource E: Example, Student Lesson Plan

Lesson Title:

Objective(s):

Materials: (What materials will you need to accomplish this lesson?)

Anticipatory Set: (What will you do to get the attention of students before you start the lesson?)

Share the objective(s): (How will you share the objective[s] with other students?)

Instruction: (What will *you* do during this lesson?)
(What will *students* do during this lesson?)

Check for comprehension: (What will you do *and* what will students be doing so that you know they are working toward achieving the objective[s] of the lesson?)

Closure: (What will you do or say to students to sum up the important points of this lesson?)

References

Atkinson, J. W. (1964). *An introduction to motivation.* Princeton, NJ: Van Nostrand.

Bandura, A. (1977). *Social learning theory.* Englewood Cliffs, NJ: Prentice Hall.

Bandura, A., & Schunk, D. H. (1981). Cultivating competence, self-efficacy and intrinsic interest through proximal self-motivation. *Journal of Personality and Social Psychology, 41,* 586–598.

Bloom, B. S., Englehart, M. D., Furst, E. J., Hill, W. K., & Krathwohl, D. R. (1956). *Taxonomy of educational objectives, handbook I: Cognitive domain.* New York: David McKay.

Bruner, J. S. (1962). *The process of education.* Cambridge, MA: Harvard University Press.

Canter, L. (1989). Assertive discipline: More than names on the board and marbles in a jar. *Phi Delta Kappan, 71*(1), 57–61.

Carr, E., & Ogle, D. (1987). K-W-L plus: A strategy for comprehension and summarization. *Journal of Reading, 30,* 626–631.

Clark, R. (2003). *The essential 55.* New York: Hyperion.

Connors, N. A. (1990). *Maintaining academic excellence in the middle grades through positive actions and attitudes.* Unpublished manuscript.

Coopersmith, S. (1967). *The antecedents of self-esteem.* San Francisco: Freeman.

Danforth, S. (2004). *Engaging troubled students: A constructivist approach.* Thousand Oaks, CA: Corwin.

Deckers, L. (2005). *Motivation: Biological, psychological, and environmental* (2nd ed.). New York: Pearson.

Edwards, W. (1954). The theory of decision-making. *Psychology Bulletin, 51,* 380–417.

Eichhorn, D. H. (1966). *The middle school.* New York: Center for Applied Research in Education.

Gagné, R. M. (1965). *The conditions of learning.* Chicago: Holt, Rinehart and Winston.

Gagné, R. M. (1974). *Essentials of learning for instruction.* Hinsdale, IL: Dryden Press.

Glasser, W. (1990). *The quality school.* New York: Harper & Row.

Greene, L. J. (2005). *Helping students fix problems and avoid crises: An easy-to-use intervention resource for grades 1–4.* Thousand Oaks, CA: Corwin.

Harmin, M. (1994). *Inspiring active learning: A handbook for teachers.* Alexandria, VA: Association for Supervision and Curriculum Development.

Hunter, R. (2004). *Madeline Hunter's mastery teaching* (Updated ed.). Thousand Oaks, CA: Corwin.

Johnson, D. W., & Johnson, R. T. (1994). *Learning together and alone: Cooperative, competitive, and individualistic learning* (4th ed.). Boston: Allyn & Bacon.

Johnson, J. (with Hinton, E.). (1993, August 15). Treat them as winners . . . and they will win, *Parade*, 3–5.

Kipfer, B. (1990). *14,000 things to be happy about.* New York: Workman Publishing.

Marzano, R. J. (2003). *What works in schools: Translating research into action.* Alexandria, VA: Association for Supervision and Curriculum Development.

Maslow, A. H. (1954). *Motivation and personality.* New York: Harper & Row.

Maslow, A. H. (1968). *Toward a psychology of being* (2nd ed.). New York: Van Nostrand.

McLester, S., Davidson, H., Brown, M., Warlick, D., Klopfer, E., Solomon, G., et al. (2003). Top 10 innovative projects. *Technology & Learning, 24*(4), 24.

Ogle, D. (1986). A teaching model that develops active reading of expository text. *Reading Teacher, 39*, 564–570.

Peter, L. J., & Ireland, C. M. (1990). *Processes of teaching.* Needham Heights, MA: Ginn Press.

Piper, W. (1990). *The little engine that could* [Miniature version]. New York: Platt and Munk.

Purkey, W. (Speaker). (1990). *The heart of teaching . . . teaching with the heart* (Cassette Recording No. ATE-90–04). Las Vegas, NV: Association of Teacher Educators.

Shanley, M. K. (1990). *Apple seeds: Thoughts for teachers.* Marshalltown, IA: Thoughtful Books Sta-Kris.

Simon, S. B., Howe, L. W., & Kirschenbaum, H. (1972). *Values clarification: A handbook of practical strategies for teachers and students.* New York: Hart.

Slavin, R. E. (1995). *Cooperative learning: Theory, research, and practice* (2nd ed.). Boston: Allyn & Bacon.

Slavin, R. E. (1997). *Educational psychology: Theory and practice* (5th ed.). Boston: Allyn & Bacon.

Weiner, B. (1990). History of motivation research in education. *Journal of Educational Psychology, 82*, 616–622.

Wlodkowski, R. J. (1982). *What research says to the teacher: Motivation.* Washington, DC: National Education Association.

Wlodkowski, R. J. (1999). Motivation and diversity: A framework for teaching. In M. Theall (Ed.), *Motivation from within: Approaches for encouraging faculty and students to excel* (pp. 7–16). San Francisco: Jossey-Bass.

Web Sites

http://www.howtolearn.com
http://www.idpride.net
http://www.puzzlemaker.com

Index

**CORWIN
PRESS**

The Corwin Press logo—a raven striding across an open book—represents the union of courage and learning. Corwin Press is committed to improving education for all learners by publishing books and other professional development resources for those serving the field of PreK–12 education. By providing practical, hands-on materials, Corwin Press continues to carry out the promise of its motto: **"Helping Educators Do Their Work Better."**